GROWING
the distance

Timeless principles
for personal, career,
and family success

JIM CLEMMER

GROWING THE DISTANCE: Timeless principles for personal, career, and family success

Published by TCG Press, an imprint of the CLEMMER Group Inc., Kitchener, Ontario

DESIGN, EDITORIAL AND PRODUCTION:	MATTHEWS COMMUNICATIONS DESIGN INC.
MANAGING EDITOR:	PETER MATTHEWS
SENIOR DESIGNER:	ELAINE THOMPSON
INDEXER:	BARBARA SCHON

Library of Congress Number: 2005905643

ISBN 10: 0-9684675-3-9

ISBN 13: 978-0-9684675-3-4

Manufactured in the United States of America

9 8 7 6 5 4 3 2 1

About this Book

Many people don't read leadership and personal development books (even though they may own a few) because they are turned off by an academic, detailed, or preachy approach. That's why, with *Growing the Distance*, we decided to present this collection of timeless growth and leadership principles in a new and uniquely approachable format.

Here you'll find each chapter — and each section within that chapter — structured with "layered" headings, summary paragraphs, and subheadings. The text is set in distinct modules, any of which can be read in just a few minutes.

What that means for you, the reader, is an opportunity to read this book in exactly as much depth as your time or interest allows. So you can browse the book and gather just the essential principles. Or you can enrich that information with all the quotes, anecdotes, and commentary that you'll find in *Growing the Distance*.

Leadership and personal growth isn't a step-by-step formula. It's not a linear "begin here and end there" process. It's as individual as we are. *Growing the Distance* uses that philosophy to provide an inspirational guide that each reader can tailor and make their own for years to come.

Contents

ACKNOWLEDGMENTS

I'm not a teacher: only a fellow-traveler of whom you asked the way.
I pointed ahead — ahead of myself as well as you.

George Bernard Shaw

Many people have made countless contributions directly to this book, to my life, or to the companies I have kept and from which I have drawn so many experiences. Some people avoid giving credit or recognition to others because they're afraid of missing someone. I'll take that chance so I can give a well-deserved thanks to the people who have helped me grow some of the long distance I have yet to travel.

I owe a big portion of my books and much of the last 25 years of my life to Heather, my invaluable life and business partner. Thanks to Chris, Jenn, and Vanessa for patiently putting up with my "Dad Jokes" and my closed den door.

Hats off to Mark Henderson and Derek Mendham, key executives in growing The CLEMMER Group along its exciting distance so far (with so much yet to come). Thanks also to Julie Gil, our "digital diva," without whose high energy and I'll-figure-it-out attitude we would not be making our virtual organization and award-winning digital dreams come true. Thanks to Owen Griffiths for decades of friendship and support for this and our many other growth projects. Thanks to Gail DiSero, Merle Dulmadge, Gail Garbe, Ofir Gil, Danielle Pratt, Patty Schachter, Cindy Sindall, Peter Strickland, Tom Tutssel, and Andrew Vujnovich and the rapidly growing number of CLEMMER Group associates for translating our ideas and concepts into action and delivering top value to our Clients.

A big thanks to Dave Chilton for years of friendship, encouragement, invaluable guidance, and outstanding example in this exciting project. I am also grateful to Peter Matthews and Elaine Thompson of Matthews Communications Design for their efforts in shaping the editorial and design of this book — and bringing my vague concept of a "browser's digest" to life.

And thanks to the many authors, researchers, sages, speakers, and leaders too numerous to mention who've blazed the paths that I've tried to point toward — for myself as much as others.

Introduction

Little three-year-old Kim had just dressed herself and was ready to head out the door when her dad stopped her. "Just a minute," he said. "You've got your shoes on the wrong feet." Kim looked down at her feet, looked back up at her father solemnly and said, "But Daddy, these are the only feet I have."

THIS LIFETIME IS THE only one we have. And now is the time to make the most of it.

We can't change our past, but we can change our future. We can't control others, but we can control ourselves. We can meet the challenges of today's rapidly changing world by changing ourselves. We can advance from where we are now to where we want to be tomorrow. We can take action — right now — and start growing the distance.

This growing process is all about developing the qualities of leadership that each of us has, regardless of our position in society or the workplace. Because how we change and control ourselves will determine the effect we have on others. That's real leadership. And that's what this book will help you develop.

LET YOURSELF GROW

All speech, written or spoken, is a dead language,

until it finds a willing and prepared hearer.

Robert Louis Stevenson, *Reflections and Remarks on Human Life*

I AM DELIGHTED WE'VE found each other. This book is written for seekers on the grow — people who are constantly looking to improve. You're clearly one of us or you wouldn't be reading this.

I've been studying, applying, and helping others to use key leadership principles from the fields of personal, team, and organizational development since the early 1970s. During that time, I've seen many people dramatically improve their lives, as well as those of their families, teams, communities, or organizations using the leadership principles we'll be exploring.

Some of these recharged leaders have developed a personal mission to help others understand and apply these life-changing leadership approaches. And what many of these "missionaries" have discovered is that those who need the most development are the least aware of it. Their unawareness is what keeps them unaware. Since they don't seek, they don't find.

At The CLEMMER Group, my development and consulting firm, we are always fascinated by the wide variance in receptivity to our development materials, workshops, coaching, or presentations. For some, it can be life-changing. For others it's a big yawn. Since the message being transmitted is exactly the same, the big difference is in the receiver's readiness to receive. I hope that our messages and your readiness come together in the pages ahead.

JUST FOR THE FUN OF IT

"Of all days, the day on which one has not laughed is the one most surely wasted."

Sébastien-Roch Nicolas de Chamfort, *Maxims and Considerations*

HERE'S AN EXCERPT FROM my firm's vision statement that explains where I am coming from with the writing style I've tried to use throughout this book:

We're having the time of our lives. Our meetings and communications are filled with humor and fun. An important measure of our corporate health is our Laughter Index, and it's high. We know that we fly highest by taking ourselves lightly. We don't suffer from "jest lag." We've developed an image of "professional light-heartedness." We maintain a professional image with strong doses of humor and humanness. We take our purpose, vision, and values — but not ourselves — seriously.

All of which means you will be exposed to my own peculiar sense of humor. Our three teenage and pre-teenage kids (Chris, Jenn, and Vanessa) feel this book should come with a bright red warning label about that. One night at our dinner table I cracked what I thought was a pretty funny remark. Chris rolled his eyes to the ceiling and said, "Dad, I hope you don't use any of that humor with your audiences. If you do," he continued, "I am really concerned about our future." Vanessa bought me a Christmas card that read: "Dad, you've always done so much for me, so I am going to put a lot of effort into your Christmas gift." The inside continued, "That's right — I'm going to laugh at one of your jokes."

It's all too easy for a development book to be like a pair of steer horns — a point here and a point there, with a whole lot of bull in between. I will do my best to keep my points sharp and minimize your need for a shovel.

And I quote...

*What is all wisdom save a collection of platitudes? Take fifty of our current prover-
bial sayings — they are so trite, so threadbare, that we can hardly bring our lips to
utter them. None the less they embody the concentrated experience of the race and
the one who orders his life according to their teaching cannot go far wrong.*

Norman Douglas; Count Caloveglia's old teacher, in *South Wind*

I'VE LONG BEEN A collector of quotations. I heartily
agree with Benjamin Disraeli's observation that
"the wisdom of the wise and the experience of the
ages are perpetuated by quotations." This book
attempts to boil down huge fields of study and
simplify centuries of leadership wisdom.
Insightful or humorous quotations (a combination
of both are my very favorites) can instantly provide the "ah-ha picture" that's worth a thousand
words. In other cases, I'll use current quotations
from books or research to reinforce the point of a
section or chapter. If I couldn't have said it better
myself, I won't make you wade through pages of
text to prove it.

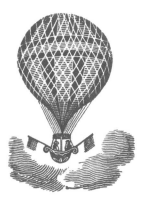

Tell me a story

Man is eminently a storyteller. His search for a purpose, a cause, an ideal, a mission and the like is largely a search for a plot and a pattern in the development of his life story.

Eric Hoffer, *The Passionate State of Mind*

Since our ancient ancestors first gathered around the campfire, we've communicated through stories. The incredible number of movies produced and books of fiction written each year shows how much we still love to be told a good story. Throughout *Growing the Distance* I have pulled from or created fables, examples, and tales. They are meant to be entertaining. I hope you enjoy them. At the same time, each story is designed to illustrate a timeless principle in that section. I hope they drive you to thinking.

WHERE'S THE ACTION?

The secret of a leader lies in the tests he has faced over the whole course of his life and the habit of action he develops in meeting those tests.

Gail Sheehy, American journalist and author

RESULTS COME FROM WHAT we *do* with what we know, not just from *what* we know. You have heard some of the ideas in this book before. The skies may not part and the hallelujah choir come down to reveal some blinding new insight to you as you read. (If you do have any heavenly visitors, however, please let me know; my contact information is on page 185.)

We all *know* much more than we *do*. We understand, but we don't act. But the key isn't knowing, it's *doing*. Successful people do those things that less successful people aren't willing to do — even though they know better. Use this book to review and reflect... then act.

As personal development speaker Zig Ziglar puts it, make this your time to give yourself a "check up from the neck up." Reflect on your actions. When it comes to leadership, knowledge isn't power. Only *applied* knowledge is power.

Jim Clemmer

At home or in the workplace, change is an inevitable fact of life. How we choose to respond to it — as leaders or as followers — determines our personal and professional growth.

The Way of the Leader

All things change, nothing is extinguished. . . .
There is nothing in the whole world which is permanent.
Everything flows onward; all things are brought into
being with a changing nature; the ages themselves
glide by in constant movement.

Ovid, Roman poet (43 B.C. – A.D. 17)

CHANGE HAPPENS. And while we can't control much of the world changing around us, we can control how we respond.

We can choose to anticipate and embrace changes or resist them. Resisting change is usually like trying to push water upstream. Generally we're quick to point to others who resist change. It's much harder to recognize or admit to our own change resistance.

Searching for stability and predictability can be one way we resist change. Stability is when everything is settled. It's when little new can happen to me. But that means there's no growth, no development, no exciting new gains that might result from unexpected pains. A condition of predictability and stability is the denial of life. It also means that the faster the world changes around me, the more likely I am to become a victim of the changes I am trying to deny.

We don't see the world as it is, we see the world as we are. If I am an unchanging stability seeker who just wants to maintain the status quo, most change is a threat. If we're constantly seeking new challenges and opportunities to grow, most changes are an opportunity.

Some people call change progress and celebrate the improvements that it brings. Others curse those same changes and long for the good old days. Same changes, different responses.

The choice is ours: We can be leaders or we can be followers.

There are two kinds of people — those who are changing and those who are setting themselves up to be victims of change.

Change or Be Changed

Every moment of one's existence, one is growing into more or retreating into less. One is always living a little more or dying a little bit.

Norman Mailer

George was 53 when he had his first attack. He'd smoked for almost 40 years, was badly overweight, had an extremely high-fat diet, and handled stress poorly. This warning shocked him into joining a smoking-cessation program. George and his wife also learned about healthy eating and improved their diets. Within a few months, he'd lost his huge stomach, was very cheerful, and full of new energy.

He was a changed man.

But slowly the memory of his big scare faded. He started having just a cigarette or two. His between-meal snacks turned into high-fat meals. As his health deteriorated and his mood blackened, he needed more cigarettes and food to cheer him up. By the time he approached his 59th birthday, he had convinced himself that he'd never had a heart attack.

That Christmas his family questioned George's return to his old destructive habits. They begged him to return to a healthier lifestyle. George defended his overeating and smoking by saying, "If I can't live the way I want, then life's not worth living." Three months later he had a massive heart attack and died.

He chose not to change. So he was changed.

SOME CHANGES APPEAR UNEXPECTEDLY as a sudden crisis. An accident, act of violence, death, or natural disaster may come out of nowhere to hit us when we least expect (or deserve) it. But most crisis points come with warning signs — if we choose to see them.

After he lost his job, a production worker at a manufacturing plant said he could "see the writing on the wall" four years ago when the company set up a flexible manufacturing pilot project to experiment with how to automate his circuit-board assembly task, among other jobs.

So what did he do during that time? Curse, pray, and organize his co-workers to decry how unfair things were? Did he try upgrading his skills while the "writing was on the wall"? He sat and waited for four years to have his fate decided for him. He chose not to change — so he was changed.

MANY "SUDDEN CHANGES" ARE really the next big step in a series of activities that we may have helped to create or allowed to continue. These changes may be the result of our failure to change our habits, lifestyle, growth patterns, or skills.

UNLESS A CRISIS ACTUALLY kills us (often it just feels like it will), it's an opportunity for us to change. It's a chance to choose a new path.

But those change choices are seldom easy. Sometimes I can be like one of those old spring-powered pocket watches: I have to be shaken hard to get me going. However, when we choose the road less traveled, we'll reflect back years later and say that, while we wouldn't want to live through the pain again, it was nevertheless an important turning point. It was one of the best things that happened to us. It seasoned and strengthened us.

Responsiveness to change is as important to organizations as it is to people. There are two kinds of organizations in today's world: those that are changing and those that are going out of business. The business and government graveyard is filled with the corpses of organizations that failed to respond to inevitable changes.

Similarly, there are also two kinds of people: those who are changing and those who are setting themselves up to be victims of change. As the world continues to march on around us, if I am only maintaining the status quo — if I'm not growing — then I'm falling behind.

GROWING AT THE SPEED OF CHANGE

What is the most rigorous law of our being? Growth.

No smallest atom of our moral, mental, or physical structure can stand

still a year. It grows — it must grow; nothing can prevent it.

Mark Twain

IF THE RATE OF external change exceeds our rate of internal growth, we're eventually going to be changed. The "ghost of crisis yet to come," similar to the third spirit that visited Ebenezer Scrooge in *A Christmas Carol*, is also as predictable. If I am a static person who hasn't developed the habits of personal growth and continuous development, I may become a statistic. "Sudden" change will catch me by surprise.

We were meant to grow. When we don't grow, we seek diversions — some harmless (if unproductive), others destructive — to fill the emptiness.

Continual growth prepares us for change. And preparing for change is like preparing for final exams. We know they're coming well in advance; with good preparation and daily discipline, there's no need to cram for the big event.

CHARLES DARWIN WAS A 19th-century British naturalist who revolutionized the study of biology with his theory of evolution based on natural selection. His most famous works include *The Origin of Species* and *The Descent of Man*. One of his key research findings was that "it is not the strongest of the species that survives, nor the most intelligent; it is the one that is most adaptable to change."

Learning and personal growth are at the heart of an individual's or organization's ability to adapt to a rapidly changing environment. The key question is, "Does our rate of internal growth exceed the rate of external change?"

Whether in the context of family, community, or organization, leaders are defined by their action — not their position.

What is Leadership?

For what we've discovered, and rediscovered, is that leadership isn't the private reserve of a few charismatic men and women. It's a process ordinary people use when they're bringing forth the best from themselves and others. Liberate the leader in everyone, and extraordinary things happen.

James M. Kouzes and Barry Z. Posner, *The Leadership Challenge: How to Keep Getting Extraordinary Things Done in Organizations*

LEADERSHIP IS A VERB, not a noun. Leadership is action, not a position. Leadership is defined by what we do, not the role we are in. Some people in "leadership roles" are excellent leaders. But too many are bosses, "snoopervisors," technocrats, "technomanagers," bureaucrats, managers, commanders, chiefs, and the like. Conversely, many people who do not have formal leadership roles are excellent leaders. In today's fast changing world, we all need to be leaders.

To lead is to show the way by going in advance. To lead is to guide or direct a course of action. To lead is to influence the behavior or opinion of others. We all need to be leaders, regardless of our formal title or role. This starts with inner self-leadership and moves outward to influence, guide, support, and lead others. The process of becoming a leader is the same as the process of becoming a highly effective human being. Leadership development is ultimately personal development. Leadership ultimately shows itself in what we do "out there." But it starts "in here." It's something that we are, which then drives what we do.

This is a leadership book. But it's not a book aimed just at those people with roles and titles such as manager, supervisor, executive, and the like. This book is about developing the leader within all of us. We'll explore the key elements to leading ourselves and others in our families, communities, social circles, or organizations.

THE MORE THE WORLD CHANGES, THE MORE LEADERSHIP PRINCIPLES STAY THE SAME

There are no new truths, but only truths that have not been recognized by those who have perceived them without noticing. A truth is something that everybody can be shown to know and to have known, as people say, all along.

Mary McCarthy, author and critic

I write these words as I sit in the office/study of my "electronic cottage." One of the reasons I love our home is because it straddles the past and the future. The front of our house looks out upon a typical suburban street with a mixture of split-levels, bungalows, and two-storey homes.

Our house is wired for business (when the kids are excited, it's just wired). Our personal computer and printer in the kid's basement room is networked with my notebook computer, printers, and our other main office computers on the third floor. We have six phone lines that enable us to operate The CLEMMER Group through phone calls, faxes, e-mail, and internet access.

My office/study looks over my perennial garden in our backyard and across a river valley to the "Pioneer Tower" — erected to mark the site of the first settlement in this area almost 200 years ago. Among these settlers were my own ancestors. They cleared the forests and broke the soil for the first farms that built this community. Horses still run in the hillside field that rises from the tower on the river bank to the farm yard.

But the more things change, the more they really do stay the same. Those settlers were powerful leaders. The principles that both drove and guided their lives centuries ago are just as relevant today. They faced up to tough choices. They lived their values. They followed their dreams. They learned and adapted. They mobilized others to build a strong community. They persisted in the face of many heart-breaking disasters. They committed their lives to a greater cause.

The reasons for their successes and failures are the same ones that determine ours today. Today's tools have changed and our society is organized differently. But the human habits and characteristics that determine our success with today's tools and society haven't changed. Our organizing systems, technologies, and the type of work we do change. But people are still people. The human elements guiding our behavior are consistent.

Leadership principles are timeless. They apply to all of us, no matter what role we play in society or organizations. It's those very personal and universal leadership principles that this book is all about.

From the center of our being, we grow the distance in six critical areas of personal development.

Inside Out

The world can doubtless never be well known by theory: practice is absolutely necessary; but surely it is of great use to a young man, before he sets out for that country, full of mazes, windings, and turnings, to have at least a general map of it, made by some experienced traveler.

Lord Chesterfield, English statesman,
The Letters of the Earl of Chesterfield to His Son

WOULDN'T IT BE EASY if we could all become leaders by following a simple sequence of steps? But the journey of personal growth means finding our own way. That's a big part of what leadership is. Life isn't one-dimensional, and neither is the process by which we grow and enrich our lives. That's why my firm, after many years of personal and leadership development work, has refined the following leadership model.

THERE ARE SEVERAL REASONS why we decided to represent the key elements of leadership in this hub-and-spoke model. One is that the growth process is centered at the hub (the "core of my being") and works outward through a variety of different paths or "spokes." The other reason is that no one path is, in itself, more important than another. And each depends on the other to complete the whole.

The leadership "wheel" formed by the hub and spokes is also circular; it has no beginning or end. It is an endless journey of self-discovery and continuous personal growth.

The distance we need to grow along each path (or leadership dimension) will differ for each of us. Some people will have greater "growing distances" for certain elements, but not for others. The goal, of course, is to grow as much as possible along all paths.

And just as the cows on the farm where I grew up never stayed milked, our growth in any of these paths is never done. Defining and continually growing our distance is the way of the leader.

The heart of this book is the next seven chapters. Each chapter is written around one of the elements in our leadership framework. The core theme of *Growing the Distance* is that strong leaders are well-rounded and constantly expanding their personal "leadership wheel" across these key areas:

- **Focus and Context.** *THE CORE OF MY BEING*: Seeing beyond what is and getting out of my "reality rut" by seeing what could be, seeing and responding to the world as I am, clarifying why I am here, and shaping my family, team, or organization's context and culture.

- **Responsibility for Choices**. *IF IT'S TO BE, IT'S UP TO ME*: Realizing that life accumulates, that choice more than chance determines my circumstance, and refusing to succumb to the highly infectious "Victimitis Virus" ("it's all their fault" and "there's nothing I can do") while helping others battle this paralyzing affliction.

- **Authenticity**. *GETTING REAL*: Changing me to change them, ringing true to who I am through exploring inner space, and gathering feedback on my personal behavior for consistency with my stated values and priorities.

- **Passion and Commitment**. *BEYOND NEAR-LIFE EXPERIENCES*: Overcoming apathy and cynicism, developing a burning commitment to our cause, moving past the path of least persistence, deepening our discipline, and hardening our habits.

- **Spirit and Meaning**. *WITH ALL MY HEART AND SOUL*: Moving beyond ways of doing things to deeper levels of being by leading from my heart and being a purposeful leader who makes meaning for others.

- **Growing and Developing**. *FROM PHASE OF LIFE TO WAY OF LIFE*: Going beyond the stagnation of stability and change management to continuous growth by cultivating the learning habit, R & R (reflection and renewal), experimenting and active learning, and developing people into what they could be.

- **Mobilizing and Energizing**. *PUTTING EMOTIONS IN MOTION*: Moving beyond manipulative motivational programs to deeper and more lasting sources of energy and power by creating high-energy environments, improving communication skills, harnessing the power of achievement, and building teams.

Blazing our own personal leadership path

The future is not some place we are going, but one we are creating.
The paths to it are not found but made, and the activity of making them
changes both the maker and the destination.

John Schaar, American sociologist

In 1985, when I was writing my first book on leadership (*The VIP Strategy*), I discovered there were nearly 3,000 Ph.D. theses on leadership in American university libraries — and probably as many books. Today, there's probably two or three times that number.

Why so many? One of the reasons for all the different leadership models, formulas, advice, etc. is that when we talk about leadership we're talking about a way of being. With billions of people in this world, there are billions of ways of being. The leadership journey is about blazing our own pathway ever upward and outward toward who we are and the life of our dreams.

In my experience, many of the people who want "practical ideas" and concrete steps to improve their leadership skills are really looking for someone to give them the answers. They want the magic solution or quick-and-easy program. They are looking for a better way of doing things.

But leadership is first and foremost a way of being — one that shows up in how we do things. There are no formulas or shortcuts to being a better and better person. Leadership is a journey of personal discovery and learning. While we can pick up valuable travel tips from others who've been down their own personal pathways, it's a never-ending process of continuously searching for and blazing our own path.

So let's get started...

GROWING POINTS

- Change happens. There are two kinds of organizations in today's world: those that are changing and those that are going out of business. There are also two kinds of people: those who are changing and those who are setting themselves up to be victims of change.

- Change can't be managed. If the rate of external change exceeds our rate of internal growth, we're eventually going to be changed. Learning and personal growth are at the heart of an organization's or individual's ability to adapt to a rapidly changing environment.

- Leadership is a verb, not a noun. Leadership is action, not a position. Leadership is defined by what we do, not the role we're in. Leadership development is ultimately personal development.

- Today's tools have changed and our society is organized differently. But the human habits and characteristics that determine our success with today's tools and society haven't changed. The human elements guiding our behavior are consistent. Leadership principles are timeless.

- There are no leadership formulas. Leadership is a journey of personal discovery and learning. While we can pick up valuable travel tips from others who've been down their own personal pathways, we can only blaze our own pathways to peak performance.

What is my **vision**? What are my **values**? What is the **purpose** of my life? These questions are at the center of our lives — and provide our

Focus and Context

> " How can you get very far,
>
> If you don't know Who You Are?
>
> How can you do what you ought,
>
> If you don't know What You've Got?
>
> And if you don't know Which to Do
>
> Of all the things in front of you,
>
> Then what you'll have when you are through
>
> Is just a mess without a clue
>
> All the best can come true
>
> If you know What and Which and Who. "
>
> Benjamin Hoff, *The Tao of Pooh*

A pig got out his pen and wandered through an estate down the country road. He went behind the stables and wallowed in a huge mud puddle. He then rummaged and ate his way through a compost heap and garbage bins near the manor house. Since there was no one around, he wandered through the courtyards and estate grounds sniffing the dirt and rooting through some of the beautifully manicured lawns and well-kept gardens.

When he finally returned to his farmyard, the hens eagerly asked for a report. "What did you see through the windows of the huge mansion?" they asked. "We've heard there are stately rooms, tapestries, fine furniture, beautiful paintings by the masters, and gold and silver everywhere."

"I saw nothing like that," snorted the pig. "There was only mud, rot, garbage, and dirt everywhere I looked."

WE FIND WHAT WE focus upon. Whether I think my world is full of richness and opportunity or garbage and despair — I am right. It's exactly like that. Because that's my point of focus. By focusing there, I turn my expectations into reality.

My focus is intertwined with the context of my life. That context is set by the people I associate with, my discipline and habits, my perceptions of "reality," my optimistic or pessimistic outlook, whether I see change as a threat or opportunity, the responsibility I take for my choices, my sense of who I am, my authenticity, my passion and commitment, my spirit and purpose, my personal growth and development, and how I energize myself and others.

Our Focus and Context is shaped by three vital questions:

• Where am I going? (my **vision** or picture of my preferred future)

• What do I believe in? (my principles or **values**) and

• Why do I exist? (my **purpose** or mission)

These questions are at the center of our lives. They are central to our taking responsibility for choices, our authenticity, our passion and commitment, our spirit and meaning, our growth and development, and our ability to energize and mobilize others. Because they are at the core or hub of our being, we put Focus and Context at the center of our leadership wheel (see page 18).

VISION IS COMPRISED OF **values** projected into the future. Both flow from our **purpose**. Vision, values, and purpose are interconnected and inseparable. Sometimes they operate like a combination lock — each twist and turn of the dial doesn't appear to do much, but when they are all lined up, the future we dare to dream of clicks open.

Another way to think of the Focus and Context of our lives is like a powerful magnet that attracts the positive or negative people, circumstances, and events. Like other natural laws (such as gravity), the law of magnetic attraction is being fulfilled today whether I am aware of it or not. I cannot change the law of magnetic attraction, but I can change the magnet. So if I want to change what's being attracted to me, I need to change the magnet and the magnetic field with which I've surrounded myself.

Look at the last five years. Have you attracted the people, circumstances, and events that you want? If not, now is the time to change what you are drawing toward yourself over the next five years.

Seeing only what is — instead of what could be — can get us stuck in our own "reality rut."

Vision

There's only one way out of a bad situation, and that's to stop believing in it. Don't make it real and it disappears.

Dan Cavicchio, *Gardens from the Sand: A Story About Looking for Answers and Finding Miracles*

Two views of reality

Joel was a realist. He prided himself in being practical and "down to earth." He was very skeptical about new ideas that changed his view of the world. "You'll have to prove it to me," he'd often say to his family or co-workers; "I'll believe it when I see it." He believed that kids today were lazy, sloppy, and untrustworthy.

Reading the newspaper after supper, he'd finish a story about some horrible crime or new violence with another comment on his pet theory that society was on a slippery slope of sin and destruction.

At work, Joel often made cynical jokes about the stupidity of management and the direction they were trying to move the organization. In meetings, he was an "abominable no man" who shot down most new ideas. "Get your head out of the clouds," he'd

snap scornfully. Then he'd prick the idea bubble with a dart like "that's never been done before" or "they'd never go for that" or "you're not living in the real world" or "that's impossible."

Denise was a dreamer. She loved to explore possibilities and try out new ideas. Change was exciting because she saw it as renewal. It was a chance to "clean out yesterday's dirt and cobwebs and start fresh." Her friends and family (at least the less critical or jealous ones) often commented on how polite, responsible, and caring her kids were. This meshed with Denise's belief that today's kids are generally a little more mature and advanced than in her own younger years.

Denise felt blessed to be living in such abundant and exciting times. Occasionally she'd clip a newspaper item about studies that showed how prosperity, health, crime, and other indicators of society's progress have been steadily improving through the decades.

At work, Denise didn't always agree with management's decisions, but she tried to understand and support the direction in which they were taking the organization. In meetings, she was an idealist who tried to encourage the team toward breakthrough thinking. When the team started complaining or feeling overwhelmed by problems, she'd often say "let's not get stuck in the past," "we're bigger than this problem," "let's stretch our thinking," or "just imagine if we could...."

WHO'S LIVING IN THE "real world?" Of course, they both are.

Joel and Denise are creating their own reality. They can both say, "See, I told you that would happen." But Denise is one of those rare, forward-thinking people — a leader who recognizes that everything we now take for granted in our daily lives was once the product of someone's fertile imagination. When flight, telephones, automobiles, or computers were first proposed, most people, like Joel, scoffed. They said these ideas were fanciful, impossible, silly, useless toys, or even deadly. And after these innovations became widely accepted, the scoffers viewed them simply as inevitable extensions of some other technology.

Joel is one such scoffer, and he's firmly stuck in his reality rut. He's so narrow-minded he could see through a key hole with both eyes. Joel expects nothing and is rarely disappointed. He is the kind of cynic author Ambrose Bierce once defined as a "blackguard whose faulty vision sees things as they are, not as they ought to be." He can't see tomorrow's possibilities just over the horizon because his head is down and focused on today's problems.

Research shows that Joel's chances of sickness and disease, depression, relationship problems, career stagnation, parental challenges, and energy loss are much higher than Denise's. He is creating the reality his vision is focused upon. The context of his values and purpose are creating the life he believes in.

YIELD OF DREAMS

Take time to dream! In each creative mind a dream takes wings and moves in graceful flow until it permeates the soul in relentless and persistent longing. The dream keeps urging "It could be." It won't let go 'til the dreamer heeds and shapes it into reality.

Anonymous

In the early 1950s, Florence Chadwick became the first woman to swim the English Channel in both directions. On her first attempt, she had been swimming for hours and was getting very near to the English coast. That's when the seas turned much colder and heavy swells developed. A dense fog settled in, blocking everything from view with a chilly, wet blanket.

As Florence's pace slowed and energy drained, her mother called through the fog from one of the small boats following behind, "Come on, Florence, you can make it. It's only a little further." But she was exhausted and couldn't go any further. As she slumped into the boat, Florence felt defeated and was heartbroken when she realized how close she'd come. Later she told the media, "I am not offering excuses, but I think I could have made it if I had been able to see my goal." On her next attempt, Florence developed a powerful mental image of the coast of England. She memorized every coastal feature and replayed those images again and again in her mind. This time she encountered the same discouraging conditions as before. But her vision saw her through to success.

Carl Hiebert also used visioning to reach his goal of being the first person to fly an ultralight aircraft across Canada during Expo '86 in Vancouver. It took him five years of planning and preparation. The 58-day adventure was marked by an emergency crash landing, severe weather, and numerous other natural and human-made challenges.

Here's how Carl describes the key role vision played in his unprecedented achievement:

"As the pavilions of the World's Fair became visible, I was surprised by how familiar they looked... then it struck me. I had seen this view many times through the process of visualization... I had pasted a photograph of my ultralight in the sky just above the cluster of pavilions, and almost every day, for the next twelve months, I had spent a few minutes staring at that picture, imaging myself arriving safely at Expo. Visualizing my victorious arrival had become the proverbial carrot hung just beyond the doubts and difficulties. It had been the incentive I needed to stay with my commitment."

A BIG PART OF Florence and Carl's extraordinary achievements came from their ability to tap into the mighty power of vision.

They aren't alone. In the last few decades, extensive research on peak performance, leadership, personal effectiveness, adaptability to change, the abilities of world-class athletes — even the healing process — clearly shows the central role vision plays in success.

Most organizations, social movements, world records, new products or services, and remarkable achievements began as the product of someone's imagination. That person had an idea, the realization of which turned into a dream. The power of that dream grew even as the dreamer was being ridiculed and told to "get real."

In 1924, Thomas Watson Sr. was heavily in debt when he came home one evening and proudly announced that his struggling Computing-Tabulating-Recording Company would now be called International Business Machines (IBM). Hearing this, his 10 year-old son, who later became a key figure in IBM's growth, "stood in the doorway of the living room thinking, 'That little outfit?'"

COUPLED WITH DISCIPLINED ACTION, dreams become a magnetized vision that attracts the people, events, and circumstances needed to achieve the breakthrough. The Joels of this world cynically dismiss it all as "luck."

THE WORD VISION COMES from the Latin root meaning "to see." What we see depends upon where we look — our focus. A dream or vision is one of the most powerful forces in the universe. Like any mighty energy, our visions can help or hurt us because they become self-fulfilling prophecies.

If we see ourselves as helpless victims of change, that's exactly what we'll be. If our attitude is "same old crap, different day," we'll get what we asked for. If we don't talk to ourselves because we don't like to deal with such a low class of person, our poor self-image won't improve. If we focus on the thieves, liars, and idiots all around us, we'll miss the saints that walk among us.

A little girl, riding in the front seat of the car beside her mother, asked "Where are all the stupid jerks today?" Her mother replied, "They only come out when your father's driving."

IF WE SEE LITTLE but frustration, dead ends, and career or family traps in our future, that's where we're headed. A skeptical "realist" like Joel lives by the philosophy, "I'll believe it when I see it." A dreamer like Denise harnesses the vision force and successfully moves through life knowing, "I'll see it when I believe it."

Being all that we can see

OUR VISION OR IMAGINATION is the center point that focuses and guides our choices, authenticity, passion, spirit, growth and development, and energy. The remarkable blind and deaf author, Helen Keller, once said, "Nothing is more tragic than someone who has sight, but no vision."

We can't leave the incredible magnetic power of vision unharnessed. Left on their own, our thoughts often pull us toward the reasons why we can't succeed rather than the many reasons we can. To increase our effectiveness, we need to actively and consciously attract into our lives what we truly want. We need to ensure the picture of our future is what we prefer, not the dark images of our fears, doubts, and insecurities that will then come true. Personal, team, or organizational improvement starts with "imagineering."

TRADITIONALLY, MANY NATIVE CANADIAN and American peoples have embarked on a vision quest as part of their passage from puberty. This typically involved a period of isolation, fasting, and meditating on an inward journey of discovery. The goal was greater insight on life's meaning and purpose for the person on the quest.

Likewise, the success, happiness, and harmony we see in our own lives depends heavily on the clarity of our vision. Rather than a one-time event, a lifelong vision quest provides a powerful focus and context in our personal, team, and organizational lives.

Clarity of vision depends on knowing what's really important.

Values

There is no objective reality.
We don't see the world as it is, we see the world as we are.

Anonymous

THE GAP BETWEEN WHAT we say we value and how we live can get pretty big. Many people don't try to do what's right; they try to guess what other people think is right. For example, when someone says it's not about the money, but the principle of the thing, it's usually about the money. The manager of a large bookstore once told me that the book they have stolen the most is the Bible.

Sean was filling out a university questionnaire to help determine roommate compatibility. Beside the questions, "Do you make your bed every day?" and "Do you consider yourself a neat person?" he checked "Yes." Later his mother reviewed the questionnaire. Knowing those answers were far from the truth, she asked Sean why he'd lied. "What do you expect me to do?" he retorted. "I don't want to get stuck living with some slob!"

Hypocrites climb the social, organizational, or career ladder wrong by wrong, all the while trying to justify, excuse, or disguise their behavior. Like Mae West in *Klondike Annie*, when choosing between two evils, they pick the one they haven't tried before.

Hypocrisy is largely an exercise in self-deception. When our acts don't mesh with our words, we are not being true to ourselves. We are not authentic.

Lack of **authenticity** often stems from a failure to recognize the values or beliefs that are really at the core of who we are. When we're not centered with a solid core, we often perceive change as a threat. It's also harder to accumulate the positive choices that vaccinate us against the Victimitis Virus and keep us from living in Pity City.

Without a strong set of core values, **passion** is weak and **commitment** is soft. We're more likely to lead our lives from the outside in, rather than the inside out. A centered leader grows his or her inner space and provides **spirit and meaning** to others.

When our values aren't in focus, our energy is easily scattered. That makes it tougher to **mobilize** ourselves — never mind anyone else. Core values provide a context for continuous **growth** and **development** that takes us toward our dreams. Our core values project forward to become our vision. How we see the world is what we project from ourselves.

OUR INNER SELVES REVEALED

It is always easier to fight for one's principles than to live up to them.

Alfred Adler, Austrian psychiatrist

OUR CORE VALUES SHOW themselves in many ways. One is at points of crisis, disaster, or adversity. That's often when our actions move us unconsciously from the depth of our heart. Any masks we may be wearing are torn off to reveal our true face.

Money is often another powerful way a person's core essence is revealed to him or herself and/or others. It's amazing to hear some people proclaim family values and then trash their "loved ones" over an inheritance. Greed is responsible for some mighty creative rationalizations. It's great to have money and the good life that money can buy. But we need to ensure that we haven't lost the invaluable things that money can't buy.

REVELATION 1:
Our self-worth

The 18th-century Scottish poet and songwriter Robert Burns was standing on the waterfront at Greenock. Suddenly a wealthy merchant from the town fell into the harbor. He couldn't swim and was quickly drowning. A passing sailor immediately jumped into the dangerous waters and rescued him. When the merchant was back on the dock, and he recovered from his fright, he put his hand into his pocket and rewarded the sailor with a shilling. A few people in the crowd that had collected to watch the drama unfold shouted contemptuous jeers over the puny fee being given to the sailor. But Burns, with a scornful smile, asked them to restrain their clamor. "The gentleman," said the poet, "is of course the best judge of the value of his own life."

REVELATION 2: Balancing work and family

A workaholic husband was on his way to work one morning. As he headed out the door, his wife said, "Harold, don't forget, the movers are coming today. Don't come back here after work."

"Who do you think I am, Dorothy?" he replied. "Don't you think I can remember that?"

After work, Harold, who had been absorbed in an endless number of hectic business details during the day, rushed home to his old house. Seeing the empty house as he pulled in the driveway, he suddenly remembered — and panicked. Stopping a boy who was riding his bicycle on the sidewalk, Harold asked, "Do you know the people that lived here?"

"Of course I do," replied the boy.

"Do you know where they moved?"

Disgustedly, the boy said, "Aw, come on Dad. Mom was right after all. She told me you'd forget!"

In GOING DEEP, IAN PERCY writes, "Most business people I know are much more concerned with the quality of their customer service than they are with the quality of their parenting and spousing." One of the executives of my firm once acted as a consultant to a highly successful company where the executives proudly declared they had the highest divorce rate of any major corporation in America. Many wore their divorces as a badge of honor to show their commitment to the company.

Yet these executives had failed to ask themselves an important question: When the company suddenly tosses them aside or they reach retirement, will they be so sure that career success is worth the cost of a broken family? Does this trade-off really represent their core values?

TELLING ON OURSELVES

About morals, I know only that what is moral is what you feel good after and what is immoral is what you feel bad after.

Ernest Hemingway, *Death in the Afternoon*

James Allen's poem is a powerful description of how our actions reveal our core values:

YOU TELL ON YOURSELF

You tell on yourself by the friends you seek

By the manner in which you speak

By the way you employ your leisure time

By the use you make of dollar and dime

You tell what you are by the things you wear

By the spirit in which your burdens bear

By the kind of things at which you laugh

By the records you play on the phonograph

You tell what you are by the way you walk

By the things of which you delight to talk

By the manner in which you bear defeat

By so simple a thing as how you eat

By the books you choose from the well-filled shelf

In these ways and more, you tell on yourself.

FOCUS AND CONTEXT

Why are we here? The answer reflects our **values** and focuses our **vision**.

Purpose

"One's prime is elusive. You little girls, when you grow up, must be on the alert to recognize your prime at whatever time of your life it may occur. You must then live it to the full."

Miss Brodie, in *The Prime of Miss Jean Brodie*, by British novelist Muriel Spark

Three women are killed in a car crash on the way home from a weekend excursion. Their souls are immediately whisked off to heaven to for an orientation session. Each one was asked, "When you are in your casket and friends and family are mourning your death, what would you like to hear them say about you?"

The first woman said, "I'd like to hear them say that I was a great entrepreneur and a terrific mother."

The second woman responded, "I would like to hear that I was a wonderful wife and school teacher who made a huge difference in our children of tomorrow."

The last woman replied, "I would love to hear them say... look, she's moving!"

A POWERFUL WAY TO uncover or strengthen our sense of purpose is to think through what we'd like to be able to say our life stood for when it's all over. The answer to that question reflects our values and focuses our vision for whatever years we do have left.

Mohammed believed that "a man's true wealth hereafter, is the good he does in this world to his fellow man. When he dies, people will say, 'What property has he left behind him?' but the angels will ask, 'What good deeds has he sent before him?'"

ONE OF MY FAVORITE annual Christmas-season rituals is to watch the movie *It's a Wonderful Life*, starring a young Jimmy Stewart as the hero, George Bailey. It's a 1930s classic that tells a very compelling story about making a difference in the lives of many others. Years ago I first rented the video after reading that a judge ordered someone who had tried to commit suicide to watch the movie.

FOR THOSE OF YOU who haven't seen the movie, the story centers on George Bailey, a young man who dreams of leaving the small town of Bedford Falls to see the world. Instead, personal and family duties keep him at home, where he becomes a reluctant community leader. Years later, frustrated by a sense of failure that culminates in a personal financial crisis, George is about to jump off a bridge so his family can collect on his life insurance policy, only to be rescued by Clarence, George's guardian angel. In response to George's bitter declaration that it would be better if he had never been born, Clarence shows him that life would have been much poorer — for his family, friends, and even complete strangers whose lives he had touched. In true movie fashion, George joyfully returns to his real life, and the financial crisis is resolved by grateful friends and family.

It's a Wonderful Life raises important questions. What voids have I filled? Whose lives have I touched? Who have I yet to touch? What bad things would have happened if I were not here? What would I want the key players in my life to say my life stood for or the difference I made? Who would those key players be? What have our lives made visible to others that, without us, would not have been seen?

Purpose is the third key element of our focus and context. It is tightly intertwined with — and of equal importance to — **values** and **vision**. All three strands work together to provide the texture and focal point of our lives, whether at home or in the workplace. The stronger our sense of purpose or mission, the stronger our **energy**, **passion**, and **commitment**.

Many people who've studied or thought deeply about what makes strong leaders have come to the same conclusion as Benjamin Disraeli when he wrote, "I have brought myself, by long meditation, to the conviction that a human being with a settled purpose must accomplish it, and that nothing can resist a will which will stake even existence upon its fulfillment."

WHAT'S REALLY IMPORTANT

He who has no mission in life is the poorest of all.

Albert Schweitzer

The legendary inventor Thomas Edison had just come through a period of exceptionally hard work and even longer hours than normal. At dinner his wife said, "You've been working too hard with no breaks. You need a vacation." "But where would I go?" he asked her. "Think about where you'd rather be than any other place on earth," she replied. Edison thought for a few moments then said, "All right, I'll go tomorrow morning." The next day he was back to work in his laboratory.

When Geoff came home late from work again, his eight-year-old daughter Tiffany was waiting for him at the door. As he walked into the kitchen, Tiffany asked, "How much do you make an hour, daddy?" Tired and stressed out, Geoff was angry with the question. "That's none of your business!" he replied.

But Tiffany was persistent. "Please daddy, tell me; how much do you make an hour."

"All right," Geoff snapped, "I make $20 an hour." Then Tiffany asked, "Daddy, can I borrow $10?"

"Forget it," Geoff barked as he stormed out of the room.

Later that evening, Geoff was feeling badly about the way he had treated his daughter. So he went up to her room where he found a teary-eyed Tiffany still wide awake. Pulling a ten-dollar bill from his pocket, Geoff sat on the side of her bed and tenderly gave it to her. Tiffany smiled weakly and took a handful of crumpled bills and coins from the drawer in her night stand. Handing it all to Geoff, she said excitedly, "Thanks, now I have $20! Can I buy an hour of your time tomorrow, daddy?"

WHAT ARE WE TO make of these stories? Edison clearly found purpose in his work. In fact, it wasn't work; it was his life's calling. Geoff, on the other hand, may have found the same fulfillment from his work. Yet both pursued their purpose to the exclusion of other things in their lives. It's tempting to judge such single-mindedness harshly, but we need to respect everyone's right to make choices according to their personal core values and unique purpose.

The real danger comes from acting without purpose. If we're not leading a purposeful life, it's easy to drift aimlessly and become trapped in our own "misery-series."

People who want very little from life and enjoy what they have can be wealthier than those who have a lot, but always want much more. And some people who just let life happen to them end up enriched and fulfilled. But drifting to a rich and full life is the exception. The most fulfilled lives are generally the most purposeful lives.

FAMILY VALUES

FOR LEADERS WITH A strong sense of purpose, balancing the often conflicting needs of work and family is a major challenge. And as you may have guessed by now, I have a strong bias in favor of family values and purposeful parenting for people who've chosen to have children.

Aside from powerful entrepreneurs or executives who build strong and lasting organizations, the legacy of our parenting is one of the key ways we can make a difference or mess up a lot of lives. The impact of our parental leadership lasts for generations — touching dozens, if not hundreds, of lives still to come.

That's why I agree with Martin Baxbaum, who wrote: "You can use most any measure when you're speaking of success. You can measure it in fancy home, expensive car or dress. But the measure of your real success is one you cannot spend — It's the way your child describes you when talking to a friend."

For parents, I believe that a key measurement of our wealth is the love and respect of our children.

Effective leaders help to keep the people around them connected and energized.

Shaping focus and context

" The historic period in which we live is a period of awakening to a commitment to higher values, a reawakening of individual purpose, and a reawakening of the longing to fulfill that purpose in life."

Robert Fritz, *The Path of Least Resistance*

Joel and Denise each led fund-raising campaigns for their respective service club and community agency. Under another member's leadership, Joel's club had raised a record amount in their last effort. Joel wasn't sure they could come close to that level again. But organization was one of his real strengths. Believing in "planning your work and working your plan," Joel set targets and efficiently established roles and responsibilities for each volunteer in his fund-raising group.

He gave crisp reports at each meeting filled with words like "outcome measurement" and "goal realization." He pushed everyone hard to meet their commitments. He developed recognition programs with rewards and incentives for those donating money and those collecting it. He organized rallies such as "Making a Difference" days.

When the fund-raising campaign was over, they fell just short of their target.

Denise knew that organization was important. She recruited someone with those skills to help her manage the fund-raising campaign. She concentrated on connecting the donors and volunteers to the difference they were making in the lives of so many people in their community.

Drawing from her public speaking training, Denise loved to tell stories about how the money they raised helped to support Lucy, who was blind, continue her education and find a job. Or she'd talk about how Ralph and his family used a counselling center to find new hope and direction after he lost his job from years of painful back problems.

At many meetings, she invited the people they were helping to come in and tell their stories. One such person, Susan, came to a meeting and quietly told of how drugs and alcohol led to horrible neglect and abuse of her three-year-old son. With the help of a treatment center funded by Denise's agency, Susan was now clean, sober, and graduating shortly from a nursing school. There wasn't a dry eye in the room.

Throughout the fund-raising campaign, Denise constantly reminded the group of their vision to build a "caring community" and improving quality of life for all. She kept referring back to their four "touchstone values" of CARE (Collaboration, Alliances, Respect, and Empathy). Donors, businesses, government agencies, and volunteers were moved and energized. They were making a difference.

The fund-raising campaign exceeded its target.

WHETHER IN OUR PERSONAL or business lives, it's easy to become overly focused on tasks and results. Within many organizations, progress and success are gauged by tangible measures like volume, activity levels, revenues, or profits. Intangibles such as energy and focus are recognized as important, yet they often fade into the background.

In *Pathfinders*, Gail Sheehy writes: "My research offers impressive evidence that we feel better when we attempt to make our world better... to have purpose beyond one's self lends to existence a meaning and direction — the most important characteristic of well-being."

Like a person who walks briskly into a room and then forgets why, individuals, groups and organizations can lose sight of their purpose. So they run faster to make up for their lack of focus. By failing to take occasional detours from the daily grind of the long journey to refocus, re-energize, and rejuvenate, everyone becomes worn down and less effective.

Leaders actively pay attention to the context and culture of their families, co-workers, or community groups. They ensure that vision, values, and purpose are alive and at the center of focus.

Within an organization, this attention to context and culture might involve keeping everyone in touch with, and connected to, whomever the organization serves. It could mean keeping the long-term vision front and center, especially when problems and obstacles look insurmountable. It might involve clarifying core values and using them as a fixed framework to guide and reinforce everyone's behavior.

It could also mean aligning an individual's personal aspirations and goals with those of the group or organization. It might involve providing the training or information to move the team's effort forward. It could mean understanding an individual's needs and serving them so they can serve customers or partners.

Strong leaders shape their own team or organization's Focus and Context (and that of their families, friends, and colleagues) through vision, values, and purpose. They help themselves and others overcome problems and get out of "reality ruts" by focusing on the possibilities. Strong leaders connect and energize people. They work tirelessly to ensure that no one loses sight of what it's all about.

GROWING POINTS

- We find what we focus upon. Whether I think my world is full of richness and opportunity or garbage and despair — I am right. It's exactly like that. Because that's my point of focus.

- Our Focus and Context is shaped by three vital questions: Where am I going? (my vision or picture of my preferred future); What do I believe in? (my principles or values); and, Why do I exist? (my purpose or mission).

- Visions are values projected into the future. Both flow from purpose. Vision, values, and purpose are interconnected and inseparable.

- Extensive research in the last few decades on peak performance, leadership, personal effectiveness, adaptability to change, world-class athletes, and even the healing process, clearly shows the central role vision plays in success.

- Without a strong set of core values, we're more likely to lead our lives from the outside in, rather than the inside out. When our values aren't in focus, our energy is easily scattered.

- The stronger our sense of purpose or mission, the stronger our energy, passion, and commitment. The most fulfilled lives are generally the most purposeful lives.

- Leaders actively pay attention to the context and culture of their teams, families, or community groups. They ensure that spirit and meaning are alive and at the center of focus.

CHAPTER 3

IF IT'S TO BE, IT'S UP TO ME

When things go wrong, it's easy to blame others. Leaders take charge by accepting the consequences of their actions.

Responsibility for Choices

> *Every day all of us make hundreds of choices,*
> *most of them so menial and habitual that they are almost*
> *as automatic as breathing. Those who live in unhappy failure*
> *have never exercised their options for the better things of life*
> *because they have never been aware that they had any choices.*
>
> Og Mandino, *The Choice*

ACCEPTING RESPONSIBILITY FOR OUR choices is not only tough; in today's society it can even be considered weird. It's much easier to blame somebody or something else.

But the happiest and most successful people — the leaders who get things done and get on with their lives — know that life is an endless series of choices. They may be victimized, but refuse to be a victim. They may visit Pity City occasionally, but don't make it their permanent home.

LEADERS CONTROL THEIR OWN destiny so fate and others don't. Leaders believe that choice more than chance determines their circumstances. Even in circumstances for which they're not responsible, leaders still take responsibility for their actions.

Leaders realize that life accumulates; the choices we make — good and bad — are like deposits and withdrawals in a bank account. Over the years, we can build up a wealth of success and happiness or a deficit of despair and discouragement.

Leaders choose their destiny by directing their thoughts accordingly.

Think about someone you know well and really admire who gets things done. Someone you'd call a real leader. He or she could be a parent, grandparent, local community leader, activist, teacher, entrepreneur, manager, or coach. How often does he or she passively accept things as they are and meekly go along with whatever life hands him or her? I'll bet rarely, if ever. Leaders don't wait for something to happen, they make it happen.

After heated meetings and many warnings to clean up the community group's problems, the director was finally fired. While cleaning out his office, he met his eager new successor. "There are three sealed and numbered letters in the top drawer of this desk," he told the new director. "I left them there as my parting advice to you. Open them in order when you're really in trouble."

Within a few weeks the new director was in deep trouble, so he opened letter number one. It said simply: "Blame me." The director did and the heat was deflected. Before long he was in even deeper trouble. He opened the second letter. It advised: "Blame the economy." He did and this bought him some sympathy and time. But a few months later, the discouraged director was in major trouble. He opened the third letter. It said: "Time to write three letters."

In the dismal streets of Pity City, there's an epidemic of the Victimitis Virus.

From Groaning to Growing

> *Oh, the holiness of always being the injured party. The historically oppressed can find not only sanctity but safety in the state of victimization. When access to a better life has been denied often enough, and successfully enough, one can use the rejection as an excuse to cease all efforts.*
>
> Maya Angelou, American author
> *Singin' and Swingin' and Gettin' Merry Like Christmas*

A 38-year-old man was at his parents' home for Sunday dinner. He mournfully turned the discussion to his many problems: "I've just left my third failed marriage, I can't hold onto a job, I'm in debt up to my ears and will have to declare personal bankruptcy," he whimpered. "Where did you go wrong?"

BLAMING OTHERS FOR OUR difficulties is the easy way out. That's why it's so popular.

A job applicant put this statement on his resume: "The company made me a scapegoat, just like my three previous employers."

In *How to Save Your Own Life*, author Erica Jong writes: "No one to blame! . . . That was why most people led lives they hated, with people they hated. . . . How wonderful to have someone to blame! How wonderful to live with one's nemesis! You may be miserable, but you feel forever in the right. You may be fragmented, but you feel absolved of all the blame for it. Take your life in your own hands, and what happens? A terrible thing: no one to blame."

Rolling Stone journalist P. J. O'Rourke adds: "One of the annoying things about believing in free will and individual responsibility is the difficulty of finding somebody to blame your problems on. And when you do find somebody, it's remarkable how often his picture turns up on your driver's license."

TURN ON ANY DAYTIME talk show and you'll find endless examples of people blaming everybody and everything for the way their lives have turned out. A little channel surfing could lead to the conclusion that we're living on the Planet of the Aches.

As long as these sad souls are playing the blame game and embracing their victim role, they are stuck in that rut. It can too easily become a rut that's really a grave with the ends knocked out. Regular viewers of these "misery-series" soon end up feeling as helpless and hopeless as the continual parade of victims.

As key players in the "whine industry," these shows reflect — and help to spread — the deadliest disease in society today: the Victimitis Virus. The virus leads to poor-little-me syndrome, a state of hopelessness and powerlessness to do anything about one's problems. Once infected, sufferers run away from personal responsibilities with excuses like "it's not my job," "I was just following orders," "I am too old to change," or "the dog ate my homework" (also the title of a great book on personal responsibility by Vincent Barry).

The Victimitis Virus is the most contagious and destructive infection ever seen on this earth, and is often diagnosed along with the Pessimism Plague. Both kill, mutilate, and destroy millions of lives every year. They are also the only lethal diseases that can be transmitted without any form of physical contact, most often spreading through one-on-one, group, or mass communications.

SYMPTOMS OF THE VICTIMITIS VIRUS include bouts of doubt and discouragement diarrhea, constant vomiting of cynicism and snide remarks, pains in the neck (or lower regions) from suspicion and distrust, hopelessness headaches, waves of nausea from pessimism and put-downs, and frequent cramps from it's-beyond-my-(or our-)control language.

Such "victim-speak" often includes statements like "he/she makes me so mad I can't control myself," "that's just the way I am," "there's nothing we can do," "they won't allow that," "I have to ....," "I am no good at....," "the system won't let us," and so on. We can all add to the list from our personal favorites.

It's very easy for entire groups to become infected with the Victimitis Virus and the Pessimism Plague. The result is that many family gatherings or meetings at work turn into "primal scream therapy" or "blame storming" sessions — about a family member's poor behavior, a missed deadline, or declining sales.

Leaders refuse to let fate or others control their destiny.

Choose Not to Lose

Whether we rise to the challenge of adversity or are devastated by it is largely a matter of choice. Ultimately, we are responsible for that choice.

Carl Hiebert, author, pilot, and photographer

IN THE PREVIOUS CHAPTER, I introduced you to Carl Hiebert, who successfully completed a 58-day flight from coast to coast in an open-cockpit ultralight aircraft. That was a remarkable achievement, but not the first time that his strength of will had triumphed.

In 1981, Carl was involved in a hang-gliding accident and broke his back. As he lay crumpled in the rubble of his broken glider, he thought to himself, "I've broken my back. I'm going to spend the rest of my life in a wheelchair. I don't think I can handle this… I don't want to live." He paused and continued his thoughts: "No… I still have my mind. I need to see this as a challenge. The issue here is not my broken back, it's my attitude. How I handle this is up to me."

From many people, that would just be a lot of brave talk. As I've gotten to know Carl over the years, I know that's who he really is. He's one of the most upbeat, positive, giving, and funny people I know. It's a joy to have him to our house or just chat with him on the phone. His conversation is full of gratitude around how lucky he's been and what great gifts he's been given.

CARL HIEBERT IS ONE of the most inspiring examples of a leader that I've had the privilege of getting to know. His is an incredible story of someone who was victimized, but refused to be a victim. Although it would be the easy way out, and we'd all understand, Carl will not catch the Victimitis Virus. This excerpt from his book, *A Gift of Wings*, shows the kind of spirit that marks a mature leader who takes responsibility for choices.

Life is not fair. We live in a world of happenstance, randomness, viruses, and cars that go crunch in the night. Each day of my life begins in pain — chronic, frustrating, relentless pain….it is my biggest cross to bear…so the issue becomes one of choice. Do I focus on the pain and the outrageous injustice of it all, or do I focus on the opportunities that are still there despite the hurt?… my wheelchair brings with it many restrictions and limitations — including most of the sports I relished in the past. Focusing on these limitations is a guaranteed exercise in frustration. The alternative perspective is that my accident and this wheelchair have given me a richer life in many respects.

FROM OBSTACLES TO OPPORTUNITIES

It still holds true that man is most uniquely human when he turns obstacles into opportunities.

Eric Hoffer, *Reflections on the Human Condition*

WHETHER WE CHOOSE TO focus on our problems or our possibilities is a key leadership issue. That's why I've been collecting examples of people who have overcome obstacles. Eventually I'd like to compile these into a book I've tentatively entitled *Against the Odds: Inspirational Stories of Hope, Determination, and the Human Spirit.* (Please visit this section of our web site if you have a story to contribute.)

Heather thinks I should include her story of overcoming the tremendous odds of staying married to me for more than 20 years.

Here is a small sample of leaders who refused to accept their circumstances or "fate":

- **Arthur Bishop** has written 9 books on military history. He started when he was 68.

- Dilbert comic strip creator, **Scott Adams**, received numerous rejections from magazines and "talent schools" before United Artists finally printed a few of his early cartoons on a trial basis.

- **Alvin Law** is a thalidomide adult who has no arms, so he plays drums and piano with his feet. He speaks to kids and corporate audiences on "There's No Such Word as Can't" (a phrase he kept hearing from his parents as he grew up).

- Major **Deanna Brasseur** started out as a typist for the Canadian Armed Forces. She went on to become one of the first female fighter pilots in the world flying F18 jets.

- A convenience store clerk I know only as **Peter** was shot during a robbery. Drifting in and out of consciousness, he could see from the faces of the medical staff in the emergency room that they had given up hope of saving his life. A nurse asked if he was allergic to anything. "Yes," he replied. The doctors and nurses stopped working as they waited for his reply. He took a deep breath and yelled, "Bullets!" Over their laughter he told them, "I am choosing to live. Operate on me as if I am alive, not dead." He lived.

- **Slav Heller** was an engineer and a successful general manager of a large food plant in Poland. Disgusted with the totalitarian regime at that time, he immigrated to Canada. He was 34 years old, had a family depending on him, couldn't speak English, and had no recognized credentials. His first job was washing airplanes for $5 per hour. Within four years he learned English, re-established his engineering credentials, and was a production superintendent recognized as an expert in his field. At age 53 he completed his MBA and embarked on a consulting career.

- **Brittany Theis** is one of our daughter Jenn's best friends. She was born with dwarfism and is much shorter than other teenagers. When kids tease her about her height she tells them, "I am small on the outside but big on the inside."

These are just a few of the thousands of leaders who refuse to let fate or others control their destiny. Leaders who take responsibility for their choices. I am inspired by their shining examples when my own "cope runneth over." Such leadership strength braces me when I want to move into Pity City, don't feel up to the task, or want to quit. I seem to forget my blessings much more easily than I forget my problems. I need to remind myself that if we can't be thankful for what we have, we should at least be thankful for what we haven't got.

It's EASY TO MAKE our own difficulties (and blame someone else); it's much tougher to use our difficulties to make us. Strong leaders such as the people I've mentioned remind us that failure is an event, not a person. To fail to attempt is far worse than to attempt and fail. But look at the bright side, if at first you don't succeed — just think of how many people you've made happy.

Choice more than chance determines our circumstance. It's all a question of focus.

Perceived Reality

"What's the world's greatest lie?" the boy asked, completely surprised.

"It's this: that at a certain point in our lives, we lose control of what's happening

to us, and our lives become controlled by fate. That's the world's greatest lie."

Paulo Coelho, *The Alchemist*

The day was a winter wonderland as our family drove through the country to a Christmas open house at a friend's home. A fresh snowfall had left the trees, houses, and barns covered with an inch of magical white powder. The day was cold, but in the brilliant sunshine the snow sparkled across the fields and glittered as it wrapped the buildings and trees in its twinkling blanket. It was like driving through a Currier and Ives painting. At the open house, I babbled on about the wonder and beauty of our 30-minute drive through the enchanting scenery. Another guest who just arrived from a 90-minute drive shut me up when he snarled, "Some winter wonderland! The slush and spray from the highway was constantly smearing our windshield. It drove me nuts. I hate driving in that crap."

WHICH VIEW IS REALITY, the slush on the windshield or the winter wonderland beyond? They are both reality. Sometimes we'll hear people say "he's not living in the real world" or "that's not reality." But whose view of "reality" are we talking about? Philosophers have argued for centuries that there is no objective reality, only perceptions. There's my reality, your reality, and someone else's reality.

Most so-called "facts" are open to interpretation and are highly dependent upon what's being read into the data. We don't see the world as it is, we see the world as we are. Which is why George Bernard Shaw advised, "Better keep yourself clean and bright; you are the window through which you must see the world."

IT'S ALL ABOUT BALANCE. I can take the attitude of "don't worry, be happy," whistle a merry tune, think positive, and focus only on the bright side of life. But if I ignore the slush on the windshield, I could end up in the ditch crushed against one of those wonderland trees with the magical snow burying my mangled body.

Problems and "ugly realities" won't go away by painting a happy face on them. But too often we get overwhelmed by our problems. We let our problems trap us deep inside our own "reality rut." As long as we're stuck there, we can't see out of the rut to the possibilities beyond.

Given the festive season and a comfortable drive in the country that day, I could easily see beyond the slush on the windshield to the beauty of the winter scene that surrounded us. I don't do that often enough. It's all too easy to focus on and curse the slush on the windshield. Dwelling on our problems rather than our possibilities comes all too naturally. We often expect the worst and then say, "See, I told you that would happen," when it happens. Too often we choose to curse the darkness rather than light a candle.

RESPONSIBILITY FOR CHOICES

CHOOSING OUR OUTLOOK

...everything can be taken from us but one thing:

the last of human freedoms — to choose one's attitude in any

given set of circumstances — to choose one's own way.

Viktor Frankl, neurologist, psychiatrist, author of the classic
Man's Search for Meaning: Experiences in the Concentration Camp,
and 25 other books on existentialism, psychology, and meaning

AN OPTIMIST EXPECTS THE best possible outcome and dwells on the most hopeful aspects of a situation. He or she believes that this is the best of all possible worlds, that the universe is improving, and that good will ultimately triumph over evil. An optimist believes no one ever ruined their eyesight by looking at the bright side of life. Research on Emotional Intelligence, Attribution Theory (see Martin Seligman's outstanding book, *Learned Optimism*), and related fields shows that optimists not only go further in life, they also have a much better time on the trip. Optimists are generally healthier, happier, and leaders in their fields.

Pessimists stress the negative and take the gloomiest possible view. They typically believe that this is the worst of all possible worlds, that things naturally tend toward evil, and that evil ultimately overshadows good. Pessimists feel that gravity is a myth — the world sucks. Highly devoted pessimists take joy from proving there is no real or lasting joy. If life were a bed of roses, many pessimists wouldn't be happy until they developed an allergy. Pessimists not only expect the worst, they make the most of it when it happens.

Which view is closer to reality? Since we see the world as we are, either view becomes our reality. We choose our outlook. We choose to be an optimist or a pessimist. As former U.S. Secretary of Education William Bennett notes: "It is a matter of choice. That is perhaps the greatest insight that the ancient Roman Stoics championed for humanity. There are no menial jobs, only menial attitudes. And our attitudes are up to us."

We may have been given a tendency toward optimism or pessimism at birth, from our upbringing, or from our current environment. But we decide what we want to become from today forward. We choose whether to fix our gaze on the winter wonderland or the slush smeared on the windshield.

CHOOSING TO LET GO OF DEADLY EMOTIONS

"Resentment is the poison I take in hope that someone else will die."

Anonymous

I am running late for an important appointment and speeding down a two-lane highway. Suddenly I come up behind a garbage truck lumbering along well below the speed limit. The highway is full of oncoming traffic, curves, and hills so I can't pass. If I start to get angry, pound the steering wheel, and really work myself into a lather about this, who is in control of my emotions at this point — me or the garbage truck?

ANOTHER MILESTONE IN OUR growth is when we accept responsibility for our emotions. We chose to lose our temper. We chose to become jealous. We chose to harbor hatred.

It's much easier to give in to the Victimitis Virus. It's less painful to believe that anger, jealousy, or bitterness are somebody else's fault or beyond our control. But that makes us prisoners of our destructive emotions. We hold grudges, let old resentments build up, and become cynical. We stress ourselves out. We stew in our own deadly juices.

Holding on to destructive emotions is slow suicide. Studies are showing that stress from negative emotions presents a more dangerous risk factor for cancer and heart disease than smoking cigarettes or eating high cholesterol foods.

A GROUP OF PHYSICIANS were tested for levels of hostility while still in medical school; subsequent research showed that those with the highest scores were seven times more likely to have died by the age of 50 than those with low hostility scores.

In another study, people who had been rated as easily roused to anger were three times more likely to die of cardiac arrest than those who were more even-tempered. If they also had high cholesterol levels, the added risk from anger was five times higher.

Reflecting on the mounting evidence that destructive emotions are deadly, researcher and author Daniel Goleman notes that "an occasional display of hostility is not dangerous to health; the problem arises when hostility becomes so constant as to define an antagonistic personal style — one marked by repeated feelings of mistrust and cynicism and the propensity to snide comments and put-downs, as well as more obvious bouts of temper and rage."

For our own health and happiness, we must exercise our choice to let go. No matter how long we nurse a grudge, it won't get better. When we bury the hatchet, we need to make sure we don't keep a shovel handy. Life is too short — and likely to get even shorter — if, like vultures, we feed on dead issues.

We need to forgive and truly forget. Forgiveness is not for them, it's for me.

Bad choices accumulate like debts. Now's the time to start reversing the balance.

Taking Account

My philosophy is taking me somewhere. The big question is where. The accumulation of equity will either be there or won't be there. Life accumulates. And I'm either accumulating debt that I'll be sorry for or I am accumulating value that I'll be happy about.

Jim Rohn, personal development author and speaker

Living in the house we've built

An elderly carpenter was ready to retire. He told his employer, a building contractor, of his plans to leave the house-building business and live a more leisurely life with his wife, enjoying his extended family. He would miss the pay-check, but he needed to retire. They could get by.

His employer was sorry to see his good worker go and asked if he could build just one more house as a personal favor. The carpenter said yes, but it was easy to see that his heart was no longer in his work. He had lost his enthusiasm and the house showed it — in shoddy workmanship and inferior materials. It was an unfortunate way to end his career.

When the carpenter finished his work and his boss came to inspect the new house, the contractor handed the front-door key to the carpenter.

"This is your house," he said, "my gift to you."

What a shock! What a shame! If he had only known he was building his own house, he would have done it all so differently. Now he had to live in the home he had built none too well.

So it is with us.

We build our lives in a distracted way, reacting rather than acting, willing to put up less than the best. At important points we do not give the job our best effort. Then with a shock we look at the situation we have created and find that we are now living in the house we have built for ourselves.
Author unknown

A man complained bitterly to the bank manager about all the checks that had bounced on him. The manager looked up the history of his account. "But Mr. Jones," the manager responded, "how can we honor your checks if you're not putting money in your account? You have to make enough deposits to cover your withdrawals."

OUR CHOICES ACCUMULATE IN our "personal choice" accounts. Depending on whether our choices are bad or good, we're accumulating deficits or surpluses with each decision we make. Here are a few examples:

- After forty, our face is our own fault. It can be etched with worry or laugh lines.

- We can have ever-strengthening relationships and support networks or grow more lonely and isolated as time goes by.

- Our career expertise and experience can build toward ever-higher levels of responsibility, choices, and mastery or we can become stagnant, obsolete, and dispensable.

- We can continuously grow and prepare ourselves for new opportunities or maintain the status quo and become a victim of "sudden change."

- Our financial wealth can be growing and providing us with confidence in our future or we can be steadily narrowing future choices and planting seeds of insecurity and dependency.

- We can keep increasing the levels of love we give and receive or become ever more distant, cold, and uncaring.

- Our reputation for keeping our word can build trust or our lack of dependability can cause people to doubt our promises.

- We can grow older and wiser as our years accumulate — or we can just get old.

As WITH AN ACTIVE bank account, few of these choice accumulations are permanent. We are continually shifting the balance of our choice account. However, the longer our poor choices are allowed to accumulate, the more time and effort will be needed to shift that balance. So we need to get started immediately. Doing nothing won't reverse a negative trend. Now is the time to change the balance in five years from now. Five years ago we made choices that accumulated into today's circumstances. Time and change march on whether we're ready or not. Five years from now will arrive. Our choice accumulations over the next five years will determine whether we look back with regret or satisfaction.

MEASURING OUR ABILITY TO INFLUENCE OTHERS

Ain't no use worrying about the things out of your control, because if they're out of your control, ain't no use worrying... Ain't no use worrying about things in your control, because if they're in your control, ain't no use worrying.

Anonymous

IN OUR PERSONAL AND leadership development workshops, my firm often conducts a "degrees of control" exercise. We ask participants to come up with examples in the following areas: (1) Direct Control; (2) Influence; and (3) No Control.

While there's often lots of debate and not always full agreement, examples of "No Control" generally include things like the weather, the economy, natural disasters, freak accidents, and the like. Of course, many other people are quick to surrender to the Victimitis Virus and declare they also have no control or even influence over the behavior of anyone else.

In most cases we have just one thing that comes under Direct Control — ourselves. However, some autocratic people fool themselves into thinking they have direct control over their kids, co-workers, or subordinates.

Our degree of Influence is clearly the largest area — and the one open to the most debate. The amount of influence I have is directly related to the strength of my Influence Index in each situation. We developed the Influence Index to help participants gauge their position with a person or group in a particular situation. In each case, when participants try to influence (or lead) another person or group towards their point of view or course of action, they need to assess their position of influence. An objective and honest assessment of that position will tell them if the time is right and they have enough strength to proceed.

The assessment is based on a five-point scale, where 1 is extremely weak and 5 is extremely strong. Using that scale, we can score ourselves in each of the following 12 areas for a particular situation:

❑ my clarity around what a successful outcome would look like

❑ my understanding of their position and win (how they'll benefit?)

❑ my persuasion and communication skills

❑ my timing and the fit of my proposed action with the situation

❑ my tone and approach (will I increase or decrease defensiveness and conflict?)

❑ my genuine desire for a win/win outcome

❑ my credibility with this person or group

❑ my passion and commitment (including persistence)

❑ our levels of mutual trust

❑ the strength of our relationship

❑ how well I've covered the bases with other key influencers and built their support

❑ my appointed role, position, and authority

A total score of 45 points or higher shows I am in a strong position to influence that person or group in that situation. A score of 25 to 44 is not very strong. I might want to wait for a better time or strengthen a few of my lowest areas (which may take some time and hard work). If I score 24 points or lower, my ability to influence is very low. I clearly have a lot of work to do if I want to increase my leadership on that issue or in that situation.

THE SEVENTH U.S. PRESIDENT, Andrew Jackson, once said that "one person with courage makes a majority." It often takes courage to use the Influence Index. It's much easier to throw up our hands and walk away muttering, "I told them, but they just won't listen." The reason they don't listen often has a lot to do with my ability to influence. My ability to influence has a lot to do with my choice accumulations. If I am going to improve my Influence Index, I will have to change my choices and get to work on changing me to help change them.

By choosing our thoughts, we choose our future.

You Think So

A little kingdom I possess,
Where thoughts and feelings dwell;
And very hard the task I find
Of governing it well.

Louisa May Alcott, *My Kingdom*

A wise old sage hosted a dinner. Toward the end of the meal, everyone was given a fortune cookie and told that they were holding their future in their hands. The guests eagerly opened them to read the words of wisdom they contained. But the paper slip inside each cookie was blank.

"Is this a joke?" they asked. "Is our fortune so bleak or so full of emptiness?" The sage replied: "That's up to each of you. The choice is yours. Many people are eager to have soothsayers predict their future. Fewer are willing to take responsibility for writing their own fortune. Your future is a blank sheet of paper waiting for you to create what is to come."

As part of her eighth-grade project "Getting to Know Me," our daughter Jenn was asked to outline her personal philosophy. Here's how she described the process of choosing our thoughts and choosing our future: "If you believe you have a good future, you probably do if you stick to your beliefs and try your best. If you believe you are going to be a failure — well, then you probably will be one. See, it all works in a cycle: If you believe, you succeed; if you bail, you fail."

THE THEME OF CHOOSING our thoughts and choosing our future is a timeless leadership principle that echoes throughout the ages. Marcus Aurelius, the second-century philosopher and Roman emperor who wrote the classic *Meditations*, said simply, "Our life is what our thoughts make it." In the 16th century, William Shakespeare observed that "there's nothing good or bad but thinking makes it so." In his 19th-century *Journals*, Ralph Waldo Emerson wrote, "Life consists of what a man is thinking of all day." In 1871, Charles Darwin wrote that "the highest possible stage in moral culture is when we recognize that we ought to control our thoughts."

Core truths are regularly rediscovered and restated for their time. At the dawn of the 20th century, William James, the American philosopher and "father of modern psychology" declared, "The greatest discovery of my generation is that human beings can alter their lives by altering their attitudes of mind."

In computer programming, "source code" consists of human-readable statements which are translated into a machine code that computers can read. Computers then execute or act upon these instructions. Our own thoughts — the beginning point of all our choices — is like our personal source code that we execute or translate into action. Our thoughts set our programming instructions.

If we continue to think like we've always thought, we'll continue to get what we've always got. Our daily thought choices translate into our daily actions. Our actions accumulate to form our habits. Our habits form our character. Our character attracts our circumstances. Our circumstances determine our future.... Taking responsibility for our choices starts with choosing our thoughts.

GROWING POINTS

- We can't choose to be victimized, but we can choose whether or not to be a victim. We must take responsibility for our actions in response to circumstances for which we're not responsible.

- Leaders aren't carriers of the Victimitis Virus. They also work to help others cure their Victimitis.

- Leaders may visit Pity City for brief vacations and to help others move out.

- Choice more than chance determines our circumstance. I choose whether to see the world through optimistic or pessimistic glasses. Either choice becomes my reality.

- We can slowly kill ourselves with our own destructive emotions or let go and live.

- Life accumulates. The withdrawals and deposits in our choice accounts build a wealth of success and happiness or a debt of despair and discouragement.

- The only thing we can control is ourselves.

- The power of one to challenge the status quo and influence others is the mightiest force history has ever known. If I am going to improve my Influence Index, I will have to change my choices and get to work on changing me to help change them.

- When we choose our thoughts, we are choosing our future.

CHAPTER 4

GETTING REAL

Genuine leadership comes from within.
It demands **honesty** and **integrity**. It goes
beyond **reputation** and **personality**;
it is a function of character.

Authenticity

> *To be authentic is literally to be your own author*
> *(the words derive from the same Greek root),*
> *to discover your native energies and desires,*
> *and then find your own way of acting on them.*
> *When you have done that, you are not existing simply to*
> *live up to an image posited by the culture or*
> *by family tradition or some other authority.*
> *When you write your own life, you have played the game*
> *that was natural for you to play.*
> *You have kept covenant with your own promise.*
>
> Warren Bennis and Joan Goldsmith, *Learning to Lead*

Why the Thumb Stands Alone

Once five fingers stood side by side on a hand. They were all friends. Where one went, the others went. They worked together. They played together. They ate and washed and wrote and did their chores together.

One day the five fingers were resting on a table together when they spied a gold ring lying nearby.

"What a shiny ring!" exclaimed the First Finger.

"It would look good on me," declared the Second Finger.

"Let's take it," suggested the Third Finger.

"Quick! While nobody's looking!" whispered the Fourth Finger.

They started to reach for the ring when the Fifth Finger, the one named Thumb, spoke up.

"Wait! We shouldn't do that!" it cried.

"Why not?" demanded the other four fingers.

"Because that ring does not belong to us," said the Thumb. "It's wrong to take something that doesn't belong to you."

"But who is going to know?" asked the other fingers. "No one will see us. Come on!"

"No," said the Thumb. "It's stealing."

Then the other four fingers began to laugh and make fun of the Thumb.

"You're afraid!" said the First Finger.

"What a goody-goody," sang the Second Finger.

"You're just mad because the ring won't fit you," muttered the Third Finger.

"We thought you were more fun than that," said the Fourth Finger. "We thought you were our friend."

But the Thumb shook its head.

"I don't care what you say," it answered. "I won't steal."

"Then you can't hang around with us," shouted the other four fingers. "You can't be our friend."

So they went off in a group by themselves, and left the Thumb alone. At first they thought Thumb would follow them and beg them to take it back. But Thumb knew they were wrong and stood fast.

That is why today the thumb stands apart from the other four fingers.

THIS CHARMING AFRICAN FOLK tale illustrates why it's so often difficult to be true to ourselves. It generally means we don't follow the crowd. Standing up and standing firm for our beliefs can be lonely and unpopular. This story helps us take a whole new look at our hands. It brings new meaning to the phrase "thumbs up."

It takes strong character to exercise the courage of our convictions. It also takes a sound knowledge of what exactly our convictions are. It's easier to have no convictions, to go along, to follow the crowd. (At least I think so. Well, yeah, maybe it is....)

Strong convictions can sometimes be confused with loudly expressed opinions. Which isn't to say that loud opinions can't come from deep convictions. But people who have deep convictions — and know themselves well — usually don't feel the need to stand on a soapbox with a megaphone bellowing loudly to convince others. This form of insecurity can be an attempt to relieve the solitude of standing up alone by dragging the crowd over to join me.

Authenticity means "ringing true to me." And it's hard to do. Getting real is tough. It's a lifelong struggle to keep peeling back the layers of my external actions to get to my inner self and discover who I really am.

Ringing true to me. It calls for ever-deepening honesty and integrity in my self-awareness and reflections. It also means obtaining continual feedback from others to see how they see me. This is essential if, as a leader, I am attempting to influence or change others. Because I must first change myself to get others to follow my example. In other words, I must build within myself an authenticity that goes beyond doing — to being.

Genuine leaders are authentic; what they do reflects who they are.

The Real Me

> *What I want for my life now is for it to be simple, without secrets, I want to be who I really am with everyone, all the time.*

E. L. Doctorow, American novelist and editor

Leadership revisited

Whether we're in the boardroom or the mailroom, all of us need to be leaders. A leader isn't just appointed; a leader makes things happen. A leader takes action.

A leader doesn't say something must be done about this, a leader does something about it. Leadership is a verb, not a noun. Leadership is action, not a position.

Leadership is defined by what we do, not the role we are in. We all need to need to be leaders, regardless of our formal roles in the family, community, or workplace.

Author and consultant Robert Cooper made several trips to Tibet as part of his research on the inner side of leadership. He quotes a wise elder who became a mentor and guide: "It is from the heart." He touched his palm to his chest. "In Tibet, we call it authentic presence. It means, literally, 'field of power.' When we live from here, from the inside, we can talk openly and honestly with each other, and say the things we deeply feel, even when it's hard to say them. We hold ourselves, and each other, accountable to our best effort in all things. We search for our calling, for the path we are born to take."

Cooper goes on to reflect on the conclusions of his leadership studies: "In essence, it is a silent sphere of energy that emanates not only from the mind and physical form but from your heart — which conveys moment by moment, the emotional truth of who you really are, deep down, and what you stand for, care about, and believe…. When you live from the depths of the heart, you walk your talk, heed your conscience, and don't hesitate to take a stand. Your voice rings true and gets heard. It is through emotional depth that we begin, for example, to discover, and commit to, the unique potential which defies our destiny and leads us to the fulfillment of our larger purpose in life."

ACTION IS THE OUTER expression of leadership. But leadership isn't just what we do. It's also something that we are, which then drives what we do.

In my firm's training and consulting work, we've found that we can teach people many leadership actions. We can teach how to influence others, how to lead teams, confront issues, solve problems, and so on. We can teach leadership *doing*. But we can't teach leadership *being*. That's an inside job. It's an unending journey of personal discovery and learning. We can guide, direct, and support becoming a leader, but we can't give anyone a pre-set formula or key actions.

Some people are good leadership performers. They can "do their leadership thing" and put on very convincing acts. But in time, superficial leadership wears thin. We eventually see through to the real person.

It's not a pretty sight. Superficial leadership destroys trust and zaps energy. People feel manipulated. They often become cynical and suspicious. In this environment, ever-stronger threats or incentives are needed to prompt others to "get with the program."

The deepest and most lasting leadership comes from the inside out. It's authentic. It's real. It's genuine.

Self-deception is often a product of self-obsession.

Hypocrisy and Egotism

The true hypocrite is the one who ceases to perceive his deception, the one who lies with sincerity.

André Gide, French writer and winner of
the 1947 Nobel Prize for literature

An entrepreneur decided it was time to give his daughter, a recent business-school graduate, a lesson "in the real world." "In business, ethics are very important," he began. "Say, for instance, that a client comes in and settles his hundred-dollar account in cash. After he leaves, you notice a second hundred-dollar bill stuck to the first one. Immediately you are presented with an ethical dilemma..." The entrepreneur paused. "Should you tell your partner?"

THE AMERICAN HERITAGE DICTIONARY defines hypocrisy as "the practice or professing beliefs, feelings, or virtues that one does not hold or possess; falseness." The word has its roots in part from a Greek word meaning "to play a part, pretend."

I have come to believe that there are two types of hypocrisy: (1) deceiving or being untrue to others; and, (2) deceiving or being untrue to myself. The first type of hypocrisy is just basic dishonesty, an intentional attempt to fool someone else. The second type is sad. It's unintentional, and derives mostly from a lack of self-awareness. It is what I call "self-hypocrisy."

IN OSCAR WILDE'S *A Woman of No Importance*, Lady Hunstanton says to Mrs. Allonby, "How clever you are, my dear! You never mean a single word you say." Some people seem to feel that leadership is about image and appearances. They try to look and act the part. They work hard at faking their sincerity. They are just "empty suits" — look good, but have nothing inside. They're about as authentic as "natural vinyl."

Everyone's "phony detectors" are getting ever-better at spotting this leadership acting. We can quickly see the difference between leadership *doing* and leadership *being*. We know when someone is "doing their leadership thing" or really being a leader.

A MAJOR CONTRIBUTOR TO the self-hypocrisy that leads me to fool myself is my own ego. If I suffer from "I-strain," I can't see myself very well. If I have a "full head of esteem," I can't separate doing leadership from being a leader. If I get on my high horse, it doesn't raise me higher (and it's almost impossible to dismount gracefully).

If I have money, prestige, or position I may believe I am a successful leader. I can head down Lover's Lane holding my own hand. I can forget that praise, like perfume, should be sniffed and not swallowed. The irony is that when we are most full of ourselves, it is then that we are least aware of how full of ourselves we are.

It's too easy to get confused by the images and appearances of leadership. Too often we see leadership as *doing* and *having*. At that level, we can easily become leadership hypocrites. True leadership is *being* and *becoming*. Authentic leadership is from the inside out. When we are true to ourselves and actively blaze our own leadership pathway, it's impossible to be a leadership hypocrite.

Our continuing mission:
self-knowledge.

Exploring Inner Space

The self-explorer, whether he wants to or not, becomes the explorer of everything else. He learns to see himself, but suddenly, provided he was honest, all the rest appears, and it is as rich as he was, and, as a final crowning, richer.

Elias Canetti, Austrian novelist and philosopher, *The Secret Heart Of The Clock*

A n ass found a lion's skin, and dressed himself up in it. Then he went about frightening everyone he met, for they all took him to be a lion, men and beasts alike, and took to their heels when they saw him coming. Elated by the success of his trick, he loudly brayed in triumph. The fox heard him, and recognized him at once for the ass he was, and said to him, "Oho, my friend, it's you, is it? I, too, should have been afraid if I hadn't heard your voice."

THIS CLASSIC AESOP FABLE shows how easy it is to play a part, to appear to be someone else. But those closest to us will eventually see (or hear) the truth. The key question is — can I see myself? Can I recognize my own inner voice? Do I listen to what it is telling me? Am I drawn into roles, jobs, or relationships that I am not cut out for? Am I following the path that society or someone thinks I should be on, or am I blazing my own path? Am I following my heart?

REPUTATION IS WHAT PEOPLE think I am. **Personality** is what I seem to be. **Character** is what I really am. Our goal should be to break down the barriers between the three until they are one. That means living my life from the inside out.

WHEN I LIVE MY life from the outside in, appearances are everything. What other people think of me and want from me becomes my guiding principle. That means my confidence and self-image are out of my control. Subject to the fickle opinion of others, I set myself up to become a victim. If I simply try to make an impression, then *trying to make an impression* is the impression I make.

Part of being a leader is to serve others; so I need to know how others see me. However, I can't serve, support, or guide others if I am not coming from a strong inner core. Only if I believe in myself can I generate believers. In Shakespeare's *Hamlet*, Polonius advises his son, "This above all: to thine own self be true, and it must follow, as the night the day, thou can'st not then be false to any man."

A more contemporary storyteller, television producer Norman Lear, provides similar advice: "First and foremost, find out what it is you're about, and be that. Be what you are, and don't lose it…It's very hard to be who we are, because it doesn't seem to be what anyone wants."

Continually peeling back the layers of who we are is a lifelong effort. It's the *becoming* part of the leadership process. Our own inner space is as vast as outer space. Like the many generations of Star Trekkers, we can "boldly go where no one has gone before" as we continue to push back the frontiers of self-knowledge. If we're going to continue to deepen and grow, it's our own never-ending discovery trek.

Leadership is built upon a foundation of trust.

Honesty and Integrity

" To be honest is to be real, genuine, authentic, and bona fide.

To be dishonest is to be partly feigned, forged, fake, or fictitious.

Honesty expresses both self-respect and respect for others.

Dishonesty fully respects neither oneself nor others.

Honesty imbues lives with openness, reliability, and candor;

it expresses a disposition to live in the light.

Dishonesty seeks shade, cover, or concealment.

It is a disposition to live partly in the dark. "

William J. Bennett, *The Book of Virtues*

Seven-year-old first baseman Tanner Munsey fielded a ground ball and tried to tag a runner going from first to second base. The umpire, Laura Benson, called the runner out, but young Tanner immediately ran to her side and said, "Ma'am, I didn't tag the runner." Umpire Benson reversed herself, sent the runner to second base, and Tanner's coach gave him the game ball for his honesty.

Two weeks later, Laura Benson was again the umpire and Tanner was playing shortstop when a similar play occurred. This time Benson ruled that Tanner had missed the tag on a runner going to third base, and she called the runner safe. Tanner looked at Benson and, without saying a word, tossed the ball to the catcher and returned to his position.

Benson sensed something was wrong. "Did you tag the runner?" she asked Tanner. "Yes," he replied. Benson then called the runner out. The opposing coaches protested until she explained what had happened two weeks earlier. "If a kid is that honest," she said, "I have to give it to him."

HONESTY AND INTEGRITY ARE key ingredients in developing trust. Trust is a key element in establishing credibility. Our credibility is at the center of our ability to influence others and provide strong leadership.

In my firm's leadership-development practice, we often ask participants to list the qualities of the most effective leaders they have encountered in their family, school, community, social, or organizational lives. Words like sincere, truthful, trustworthy, reliable, principled, and genuine are usually on the list. These characteristics are the hallmarks of strong leaders.

There's lots of evidence to support author Lance Secretan's belief that "we are suffering from truth decay." In a financial management column on taking a loan to invest more money in mutual funds, a former politician advised: "If your real estate falls in value to the point where the home-equity loan is greater than the worth of your house, you can always take a walk. Then it's the bank's problem." How's that for honesty and integrity? Does he sound like a leader?

Every day we hear about (or personally experience) broken promises, cheating, "shaving the truth," cutting corners, or failing to follow through. Mark Twain advised us to "always do right. This will gratify some people and astonish the rest." Winston Churchill adds: "People occasionally stumble over the truth, but most pick themselves up and hurry off as if nothing happened."

HONESTY AND INTEGRITY ARE among the most frequently cited leadership values. But some people seem to feel it's something you can slip on and off like clothing. They will speak of specific codes of behavior according to context — personal, professional, or business — as if different suits of honesty are put on according to the situation. This shows "doing honesty" rather than being honest. It's no more than putting on an honest *act*. This is, of course, essentially dishonest. But people quickly see through it and, as a result, ascribe to *all* our behavior the lowest level of honesty and integrity — our dirtiest clothes.

That's one reason to be consistently honest. Another is the internal confusion that "situational honesty" can create: which is the real me? How can changeable honesty ring true to me?

PASSING THE TEST

OUR TRUE CHARACTER IS often revealed by how well we resist the forces of fear and greed. In times of fear we often face great difficulty and disaster. Or we might have huge opportunities for financial, career, power, or other big gains. How we deal with either situation, when the stakes are high, reveals our true selves. The choices we make during those intense moments of truth expose the depth of our character. Do we "do our honesty and integrity thing" when it's convenient or just when we think others are watching? Or are we honest only to the extent that no one's found out otherwise?

"Don't let me catch you doing that again," parents and other authority figures will sometimes say — often encouraging their charges to undertake lively games of "catch me if you can." But honesty and integrity are developed from the inside out.

Abraham Lincoln said it well in reflecting on his approach, which he explained as: "I do the best I know how, the very best I can; and I mean to keep on doing it to the end. If the end brings me out all right, what is said against me will not amount to anything. If the end brings me out all wrong, ten angels swearing I was right would make no difference."

Ringing true to me means going beyond just what I say or do. It involves listening to what my inner voice tells me about how I *feel* about what I've said or done.

ONE WAY TO MEASURE OUR INTERNAL levels of honesty and integrity is to look at how much we trust others. Since we see the world as we are, any feelings I have that people are basically dishonest and can't be trusted may be revealing more about me than them. Indeed, one of the hazards of lying is not just that people won't believe us, it's also that we won't believe anyone else.

I judge myself by my intentions.
Others judge me by my actions.

The Eye of the Beholder

Hearing "reflective back talk" from friends, colleagues, spouses, and significant others allows us to "true" ourselves in relation to their perceptions. With this input we can integrate our internal conversations with data from the external world to enrich the process of knowing ourselves better.

Warren Bennis and Joan Goldsmith, *Learning to Lead*

An elderly gentleman went to the doctor with a complaint about a gas problem. "But," he told the doctor, "it really doesn't bother me too much. When I pass gas it never smells and is always silent. As a matter of fact," he said triumphantly, "I've passed gas at least 10 times since I've been here in your office. And you didn't even know it."

"I see," the doctor replied as he examined him. When he was finished, he wrote a prescription and handed it to his patient. "Take these pills three times a day and come back to see me next week," he instructed.

The next week the gentleman was back. "Doctor," he exclaimed, "I don't know what medication you gave me, but now my gas... although still silent... stinks terribly!"

The doctor retorted, "Good! Now that we've cleared up your sinuses, let's work on your hearing."

AN EXTREMELY USEFUL STEP IN leadership development is seeing ourselves as others see us. So we need to understand their perceptions of our behavior.

My effectiveness in leading, relating to, or working with others is highly dependent on their perceptions of me. I may not agree with what they see, but their perception is my reality. Those around me have an opinion of who they think the real me is. Their perceived "truth" becomes the way they treat me. Their perception forms their part of the reality of our relationship.

IN WORKING WITH INDIVIDUALS, teams, and organizations to improve their effectiveness, I've often found the subject of perceptions to be the most problematic. For example, we tend to define levels of service or quality through our own eyes and values. But that may not be the way our customers or partners define it. There is no objective definition. There is only the reality that I see, you see, he sees, or she sees.

Our personal perception is our personal reality. There's no accounting for taste. Everyone forms his or her own opinion, no matter how wrong we may think it is. If we're going to improve the service or quality delivered, we first need to understand how those we're serving, or producing for, perceive service or quality.

Like beauty — or service, quality, honesty, or integrity — leadership is in the eye of the beholder. I judge myself by my intentions. Others judge me by my actions. My intentions and the actions that others see may be miles apart. Unless I know that, I am unlikely to change my actions or try to get others to see me differently. I can become trapped in their reality and get very frustrated when they don't respond to me as I'd like.

HOW OTHERS SEE ME

GETTING FEEDBACK FROM OTHERS on our personal behavior is tough. It often hurts. The truth may set me free, but it will likely make me miserable first.

When we get feedback, we nod our heads in agreement with the positive and supportive statements that agree with our own views. But when it comes to our weaknesses or improvement areas, we take those to heart — often too much to heart. We can get 10 rave reviews for work we've done and only one critical comment. But it's the one comment that hurts. And if we're not careful, we can let that comment fester into self-doubt and a loss of confidence.

The result? Truths that may correct our less productive habits become the truths we prefer not to hear. That's human nature. What stunts our personal growth and gets us stuck in a rut is when we refuse to hear any more of it. As a parent or a boss — or appointed leader of any type — it's too easy to hide behind our position and avoid feedback.

The wider the gap between our own perceptions of areas to improve and the feedback we're getting, the more we may experience what's been called the "SARAH" response. A model used in grief counseling, SARAH is an acronym that can also be used in understanding the stages we experience in response to criticism — Shock, Anger, Resentment, Acceptance, and Help. When I get open and honest feedback on how others perceive me, I may be *shocked, angry,* and *resentful*. But unless I *accept* their perceptions as being those of the real me (their reality of me), I'll never progress to the final stage of self-*help* — that is, seeking help from others in taking action on the feedback and making needed changes.

HUMAN NATURE IS SUCH that we are usually able to size up everyone but ourselves. As painful as it can be, feedback is a major factor in leadership development. It helps us to size up and see ourselves as others see us. We may not agree with the perceptions of others, but unless we know how others perceive us, we stand little chance of improving our relationships with others and our effectiveness in dealing with them. Feedback also gives us an opportunity to reflect on our behavior from an objective point of view. It provides outside perspectives on the exploration of our inner space.

Of course, not all feedback is valid and helpful. Ultimately, I have to decide what fits and what doesn't. I have to choose the feedback that rings true to me.

According to an ancient story, a man once approached Buddha and began to call him ugly names. Buddha listened quietly until the man ran out of insults and had to pause for breath.

"If you offer something to a person and that person refuses it, to whom does it belong?" asked Buddha.

"It belongs, I suppose, to the one who offered it," the man said. Then Buddha said, "The abuse and vile names you offer me, I refuse to accept."

The man turned and walked away.

Leaders don't seek to change others,
but to change themselves.
They become models of change for others.

Leading by Example

"We must be the change we wish to see in this world."

Mahatma Gandhi, Indian nationalist and spiritual leader
who developed the practice of nonviolent disobedience that forced
Great Britain to grant independence to India in 1947

When I was young and free and my imagination had no limits, I dreamed of changing the world.

As I grew older and wiser, I discovered the world would not change, so I shortened my sights somewhat and decided to change only my country. But it, too, seemed immovable.

As I grew into my twilight years, in one desperate attempt, I settled for changing only my family, those closest to me, but alas, they would have none of it.

And now as I lie on my deathbed, I suddenly realize if only I had changed myself first, then by example I would have changed my family. From their inspiration and encouragement, I would have been able to better my country and, who knows, I may have even changed the world.

Anonymous epitaph written on a tomb at Westminster Abbey

LIKE MANY PEOPLE, I'm often tempted to think how I'd like to change the people around me — my wife, my kids, my associates — the list is endless. But changing others is not the place to start. The place to start is with changing me.

The Nobel Prize-winning physicist Albert Einstein once observed that we can't solve a problem with the same type of thinking that created it. The same principle applies to influencing and leading people around us. I can't influence others to change what they're doing with the same behavior that contributed to their current behavior.

The more time I've spent with others who I'd like to improve or change, the more this principle applies to me. Something I've been doing, or failing to do, has contributed to their current behavior patterns. If I am going to change their behavior, I will need to change my behavior. To change them, I need to change me. As the 18th-century French writer Francois Fenelon put it, "We can often do more for others by correcting our own faults than by trying to correct theirs."

WHAT STANDS IN THE way of this key leadership principle is the common (and mistaken) belief that we can control others. It's an easy trap to fall into — particularly if I am the boss, parent, owner, teacher, coach, project leader, director, or in some similar position of authority. But the fact is that as long as I try controlling others through a position of power, I will always be stuck at the superficial level of "doing my leadership thing."

It is only when I give up trying to control that I am ready to move to the deeper levels of "leadership being" (and hence greater effectiveness as a leader). I can then shift my focus to influencing and guiding others by what I do as well as by what I say.

To *create* something we must *be* something. For example, becoming a parent is easy; *being* one is tough. We can't teach our kids self-discipline unless we *are* self-disciplined. We can't help build strong organizational teams unless we are strong team players ourselves.

This timeless principle applies to virtually every facet of our lives. We can't help develop a close community if we're not a good neighbor. We can't enjoy a happy marriage if we're not a loving partner. We won't have a supportive network of friends or colleagues until we're a supportive friend or collaborative colleague.

In *The Heart Aroused: Poetry and Preservation of the Soul in Corporate America*, David Whyte writes that "All things change when we do." Gautama Chopra elaborates: "By changing our beliefs, our perceptions, we cause our experience to change, and in this way we change the world around us. There is no true boundary or limit to the self; there is no separation from the world that encircles us. When we master the forces within, we influence the forces without."

In MY FIRM'S LEADERSHIP development work, we use a simple exercise to help people see the connection between changes they'd like to see in others and those they need to make in themselves:

Draw a line down the middle of a page. Title the left column "Changes I'd Like Them to Make." List the four or five biggest changes you'd like to see in others.

OK, that's the easy part. Now title the right column "Ways I Can Exemplify These Changes." Here, write down the ways you can influence "them" with your personal behavior. Difficult, isn't it? Of course it is — because it forces us to acknowledge all those things we have or haven't been doing to influence their behavior.

It's much easier to be a victim here, to blame others for their behavior and refuse to accept any responsibility at all. But how honest and true is that — really? I may need more feedback from them to clearly see my role in their behavior. I probably need to reflect further and deeper on our relationship. Is my Influence Index weak? (See page 59 for a description of the Influence Index.)

The big (and often painful) leadership question is: "What do I need to change about me to help change them?" Instead of just wishing for a change of circumstance, I may need a change of character.

FOLLOWING THE LEADER IN ME

We judge ourselves by what we feel capable of doing,

while others judge us by what we have already done.

Henry Wadsworth Longfellow

MOST OF US PUT LEADING by example high on the list of key leadership characteristics. We use phrases like "walking the talk" or "connecting the video with the audio" to express this core leadership concept. That's authenticity.

We recognize real leadership when we see it in others. What we often don't recognize is our own behavior reflected back to us. Children will act like their parents, despite attempts to teach them otherwise. For example, parents who have little interest in personal growth and development will find their children following their example — regardless of a teacher's encouragement. In the workplace, teams act like their leaders despite all attempts to train them otherwise. If a leader is indifferent to, say, customer service, that's what customers will experience when dealing with team members. Or family members may feel unappreciated, despite our feelings (especially if they're unexpressed) of how much they mean to us.

GOOD INTENTIONS ARE USELESS if they stop there. Unless we act on them, they're nothing more than warm, fuzzy thoughts in our heads. When it comes to leadership, the messenger must be the message.

The biblical story of the Good Samaritan would have no meaning if all he did was look with sympathy at the badly wounded traveler lying by the road. He *acted* on his compassion and made a difference. One of the biggest differences between most people and authentic leaders is action. Real leaders make it happen.

GROWING POINTS

- Leadership isn't just what we do, it's also something that we are, which then drives what we do. The deepest and most lasting leadership comes from the inside out. It's authentic. It's real. It's genuine.

- There are two types of hypocrisy: (1) deceiving or being untrue to others; and (2) deceiving or being untrue to ourselves. The first type of hypocrisy is detestable. It's an intentional attempt to fool someone else. The second type is sad. It's a lack of self-awareness. It's "self-hypocrisy."

- Reputation is what people think I am. Personality is what I seem to be. Character is what I really am. Our goal should be to blur the lines between the three until they are one and the same.

- Honesty and integrity are key ingredients in developing trust. Trust is a key element in establishing credibility. Our credibility is at the center of our ability to influence others and provide strong leadership.

- Leadership is in the eye of the beholder. I judge myself by my intentions. Others judge me by my actions. Feedback gives me another opportunity to reflect on my behavior from the viewpoint of others.

- It's not about changing them, it's about changing us. That starts with changing me. I can't influence others to change what they're doing with the same behavior that contributed to their current behavior.

- Good intentions are useless if they stop there. One of the biggest differences between most people and authentic leaders is action. Real leaders make it happen.

CHAPTER 5

BEYOND NEAR-LIFE EXPERIENCES

Successful people are energized by a love
for what they do because it brings them
ever closer to who they are.

Passion and Commitment

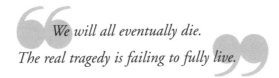

We will all eventually die.
The real tragedy is failing to fully live.

"How many people work for
your company?"

"Oh, about half."

"I think you're confusing me
with someone who cares."

"The most dangerous place
in this organization is at the
exit door around quitting time.
You'll get trampled."

"Working is like a nightmare.
I'd like to get out of it,
but I need the sleep."

"I used up all my sick days,
so I phoned in dead."

"I've developed a new philosophy: I
only dread one day at a time."

"I feel better now that I've
given up all hope."

THESE EXAMPLES OF "victim speak" are typical of the widespread apathy and cynicism that exists throughout society today. Passionate people who take responsibility for their choices don't talk like this. Family, community, team, and organizational leaders who make a difference don't consistently feel this way. Sure, we all make occasional trips to Pity City or have our "doubt days." But highly effective people — leaders — have a passion for life and a deep commitment to their work or cause (often the same thing).

Passion is love. It is pumped from our heart. It is the life energy that circulates through our lives. Love is the strongest human emotion and spirit that most deeply touches and moves us.

Our passion for what we do — or our lack of it — tells us if we're in the right place. To be passionate about our work, that work has to keep moving us ever closer to expressing who we truly are. The more closely "who we are" is aligned with "what we do," the deeper is our passion and commitment. When we love what we do, we never have to work again. We need to do more than just get a job, we need to get a life.

We can't impassion others about life or their work if we don't feel passionate about ours. Leadership charisma and energy flow directly from our personal passion and commitment. These qualities determine how others respond to our influence and leadership efforts.

The depth of our commitment determines the length of our persistence in overcoming resistance. The deeper our commitment, the deeper the reservoir of self-discipline and will power we have to draw from.

"Dead-end job" is a term most often used by dead-end people.

Uprooting apathy and cynicism

The opposite of love is not hate, it's indifference.

The opposite of art is not ugliness, it's indifference.

The opposite of faith is not heresy, it's indifference.

And the opposite of life is not death, it's indifference.

Elie Wiesel, French-American writer and
1986 Nobel Peace Prize winner

Jack and Elizabeth are in their mid-seventies and love life. They had fulfilling careers and raised three children who now have families of their own. There aren't enough hours in the day for all they like to do. Walking, swimming, traveling, volunteer work, community service club activities, family gatherings, hobbies, and reading keep them very busy. Jack has been taking a few university courses in religion, philosophy, and literature. Elizabeth has just been certified as a master gardener.

When they can squeeze it in (and they feel emotionally up to the challenge), Jack and Elizabeth try to help out their neighbors, the Reddens, who are about 10 years younger. Howard Redden is practically a shut-in with his ailing heart and numerous other health problems. He and his wife, Sylvia, spend most of their waking hours watching television and snarling at each other. Their children visit or call just often enough to feel that they've fulfilled their family duties.

Conversations with the Reddens consist mostly of listening to their outpourings of bitterness, vicious gossip, complaints about their health and boredom — and lots of blaming governments, their kids, and fate for their many problems and ailments.

IT'S INSPIRING TO BE with those optimists in their sixties, seventies, eighties, or even nineties who are excited about some new venture or interest.

Too many people let their disappointments and cynicism slowly extinguish their life spark. When they reach their senior years, they are bitter and jaded. Their dead spirits rattle in bodies that haven't been laid to rest yet. It's sad to see people who are putting in time until retirement. They hate, or just tolerate, their work, as they bide their time waiting for life to begin. They put off living and slowly die in the process. If they reach retirement, they're left wondering, "Is this all there is? Is this what life is all about?"

"How long have you worked here?" "Ever since my boss threatened to fire me."

Far too many people have retired mentally even if, physically, they still show up for work. Others have resigned their jobs but still go through the motions and are on the payroll. Often these are the same people who complain that they aren't paid what they're really worth — and should be thankful that they aren't.

On-the-job-retirees who waste their lives in a "dead-end job" they don't enjoy aren't making a living, they're making a dying. They are slaves, no matter how much money they make, status they achieve, or power they wield.

STUDIES OF THRIVING PEOPLE and their successful career paths show that the types of jobs they have had is much less important than the type of person they are. There are no dead-end jobs, but there are dead-end people. Unsuccessful people in unfulfilling jobs often make the mistake of thinking that they are working for someone else.

Apathy and cynicism usually take root early in life. If left unchecked through to middle age, they lead to bitterness, lack of energy, health problems, depression, and related difficulties. A public opinion poll taken by the National Opinion Research Center found that over half of all adults in their twenties rate their lives as "exciting." Once people reach their forties this slips to 46 percent. At sixty it falls to 34 percent.

Albert Schweitzer, the Noble Prize-winning French philosopher, physician and musician, fervently believed that "the tragedy of life is what dies inside a person while they live." As the years slide by, a growing number of people don't really live, they merely exist — trapped in their lives of quiet desperation. "Just getting by" is as dangerous as resting in the snow on a frigid winter night; our passion and spirit dozes off and dies in our sleep.

Intellectual ability is important. But leadership is more about the heart than the head.

The power of passion

A passionate interest in what you do is the secret of enjoying life, perhaps the secret of long life, whether it is helping old people or children, or making cheese, or growing earthworms.

Julia Child, American cookbook author and television personality

The French call it *joie de vivre*, which means joy or love of life. And at my firm, we wrestled long and hard with putting into words the core values that define the kind of organization we want to be. Passion is the first cornerstone of our four core values. That means creating an environment brimming with joy of life, being passionate and having fun. We've found that a positive outlook is contagious. We strive constantly to give and get deep meaning from our work. We experience life with an ever-increasing depth. We nurture the hearts and souls of each other and those we serve.

We celebrate our successes along the way. We cultivate the seemingly unnatural (but vital) skill and habit of appreciating and being thankful for what we have and what we've accomplished. We don't just focus on the mountain of unattained goals yet to be climbed, we periodically stop to enjoy the view from the vantage points we've reached.

We believe that organizations, systems, processes, and technology serve people — not the other way around. We love and celebrate the richness of life and infinite human potential in the services we provide and the way we live.

A teacher was discussing a picture of a family with her first-grade class. One little boy in the picture had different color hair and skin than the other family members. One student suggested that he was adopted. A little girl, Jenny, chimed in, "I know all about adoptions because I was adopted."

"What does it mean to be adopted?" asked another first grader.

"It means," answered Jenny, "that you grew in your mommy's heart instead of her tummy."

THE AUTHOR AND POET Samuel Ullman wrote that "age may wrinkle the face, but lack of enthusiasm wrinkles the soul." (Now there's a scary picture — just imagine the hordes of leathery, shriveled souls of all the apathetic people in the world today.) Enthusiasm is a word that comes from ancient Greek, meaning "having the god within." Enthusiasm, passion, and love are key drivers in our lives. When we connect with our inner spirit we feel the most intensely alive. During these moments, our inner voice whispers, "this is the real me."

PASSION AND LOVE ARE affairs of the heart, not the head. Because as much as we might like to think otherwise, we aren't entirely rational creatures.

Take parenting, for example. Many of us have experienced days when it seems that the decision to become a parent was irrational to the point of insanity. In fact, on those "doubt days," it's easy to understand why some animals eat their young.

Humans use thinking and reasoning to solve problems and make plans. But it's our hearts more than our heads that move us. Most so-called "rational thinking" is merely a process of justifying actions that start with our feelings. We often make decisions that "feel right" then start looking for the "facts" to support them.

In many organizations, what's often called leadership is really management. Activities such as planning, analysis, problem solving, strategy, process improvement, goal setting and measurement are all critical. And they call for good intellectual abilities. But for all their importance, they don't add up to leadership.

Leadership is emotional. Leadership deals with feelings. Leadership is made of dreams, inspiration, excitement, desire, pride, care, passion and love. The areas of our lives where we show the strongest leadership — including our communities, families, organizations, products, services, hobbies and customers — are where we're most in love.

When we're passionate about what we do, we can stop working and start living.

Labor of love

"My definition of self-actualization is that when you are confused about the difference between work and play."

Ken Blanchard, leadership author and consultant

To STOP WORKING AND start living means I need to continually clarify what really turns me on in a career, and where I want to take my life. Then I need a clear picture of the ideal job that expresses my unique talents and character.

Our work can just be a job or the canvas that allows us to paint a rich and textured portrait of our deeper selves. It inspires us to draw forth our deepest creativity. Through our lifework, we can paint the many facets of our being. The entrepreneur and business consultant in me gives a big "yes" to American pop artist Andy Warhol's assertion that "being good in business is the most fascinating kind of art."

Most highly paid professionals and wealthy entrepreneurs don't start with the goal of getting rich. People in love with money, fame, and "success" are among the saddest and unhappiest souls on earth. If they're driven hard enough, many end up with the wealth they love. But they usually hate their emotional poverty and despise themselves as much as their associates and family often do. Money can be a powerful tool or a well-deserved result. It's usually destructive when it's a goal in itself. When we do what we love and get really good at it, the money will follow.

Years ago I worked in a company with a powerful and emotionally intelligent CEO. A favorite motto of his was, "If you love what you're doing, you never have to work again." The wisdom of those words has had a strong and lasting effect on me. I hate work. It really is a disgusting four-letter word. Hard work is why I left the family farm. Whenever a job has started to feel like work, I quit. Fortunately, that's only been a few times in the last three decades. I've put years of 60- or 70- hour weeks into my career, but rarely has it felt like work.

know I am in the perfect job if I am being well paid for something I'd gladly do for free if nobody was willing to pay me. I was an unpaid speaker and writer for a few years. Of course, in those early years I was getting paid about what I was worth. Eventually I became a "good-for-nothing" speaker and writer. Finally I could charge for doing what I love.

I once led a leadership development discussion group with a group of university presidents. As we discussed passion and commitment, a consensus emerged that today's society has robbed many people of their pride-of-craft. This group of leading academics concluded that universities have been major contributors to the problem. They have helped build a job-class system that puts many white-collar professionals ahead of blue-collar tradespeople and technicians. But we all agreed that a highly skilled mechanic who loves his or her work and is continually growing and developing in it is a much stronger and more productive leader than a doctor who feels trapped in a system he or she despises.

I've met cleaners, security guards, bus drivers, and other people in low-skilled, low-paying jobs who love what they do and make strong contributions to their organizations and society. As the highly passionate American civil rights leader Martin Luther King Jr. put it, "If a man is called a street sweeper, he should sweep streets even as Michelangelo painted, or Beethoven composed music, or Shakespeare wrote poetry. He should sweep streets so well that all the hosts of heaven and earth will pause to say, here lived a great street sweeper who did his job well."

WE ALL HAVE OUR DOUBT DAYS when we're not sure we're in the right job. But our jobs aren't work unless those doubt days become as routine as getting up in the morning. If my work has become work, I've lost the passion. If I'd rather be doing something else, I need to go do it.

Life is too short to give in to the Victimitis Virus and get stuck in the rut of a meaningless job; wishing and hoping I win the lottery, my fairy-job mother magically appears, or I can just hang in there. Meaningful work goes well beyond *what* I do for a living; it joyfully expresses what I do *with* my living.

It's easy to talk about change.
Making it happen requires a

Burning commitment

"The longer I live, the more I am certain that the great difference between the feeble and the powerful, between the great and the insignificant is energy-invincible determination — a purpose once fixed, and then death or victory. This quality will do anything that can be done in this world."

Sir Thomas Buxton

During the 1980s, the Milliken textile company dramatically improved its customer service, product quality, and financial performance through an intense quality-improvement effort. They eventually won a national quality award in recognition of their success.

To promote the improvement process, office and factory walls were plastered with quality slogans and everyone wore gold lapel pins with the word "quality" emblazoned on them. Very early one morning, at the height of their drive for higher quality, CEO Roger Milliken arrived ready to address a team meeting in one of the manufacturing plants as it was coming off the night shift. The manager who met him asked, "Where's your quality pin?" Roger looked down at his lapel, smacked his forehead, and said, "Oh my God! I must have left it on my pajamas."

ROGER MILLIKEN'S RESPONSE IS an example of either very fast thinking or a remarkable commitment to the cause of quality improvement! Such burning commitment to a cause is the hallmark of passionate and highly effective leaders. There's no apathy. There's no doubt about where the leader stands and where he or she is going. As the growing research on Emotional Intelligence clearly shows, a strong point of view and a burning desire to see things through is worth dozens of IQ points.

Ella Wheeler Wilcox's poem captures the spirit of passionate commitment found in highly effective leaders:

Will

There is no chance, no destiny, no fate,

Can circumvent or hinder or control

The firm resolve of a determined soul.

Gifts count for nothing; will alone is great;

All things give way before it, soon or late.

What obstacle can stay the mighty force

Of the sea-seeking river in its course,

Or cause the ascending orb of day to wait?

Each well-born must win what it deserves.

Let the fool prate of luck. The fortunate

Is he whose earnest purpose never swerves,

Whose slightest action or inaction serves

The one great aim. Why, even Death stands still,

And waits an hour sometimes for such a will.

IN THE ORGANIZATIONAL WORLD, various types of so-called "change management" programs have become very fashionable. Yet research shows consistently that over half of them fail. Like diets and New Year's resolutions, it's easy to declare excitedly a bold new world at the start of a major change effort. But the real test comes 12, 18, or 24 months later. Rare is the individual, team, or organization still as intensely committed to the cause at that point as they were in the beginning.

Where there's a successful, long-term change or improvement effort underway, you'll always find highly committed leaders. Many people pay lip service to change. Some can even get quite passionate about the *need* for improvement. But only a handful make the leap from lip service to lifestyle change. There are canyon-sized gaps between saying and doing and, ultimately, being. The depth of our passion and commitment determines the intensity of our involvement.

Success is rarely easy or quick. It is the product of consistent effort, repeatedly applied.

Persistence goes the distance

Hang in there! is more than an expression of encouragement to someone experiencing hardship or difficulty; it is sound advice for anyone intent on doing good in the world. Whether by leading or prodding others, or improving oneself, or contributing in the thick of things to some larger cause, perseverance is often crucial to success...

Much good that might have been achieved in the world is lost through hesitation, faltering, wavering, vacillating, or just not sticking with it.

William J. Bennett, *The Book of Virtues*

In 1914, Thomas Edison's factory in West Orange, New Jersey, was virtually destroyed by fire. Although the damage exceeded $2 million, the buildings were insured for only $238,000 because they were made of concrete and thought to be fireproof.

Much of Edison's lifework went up in smoke and flames that December night. At the height of the fire, Edison's 24-year-old son, Charles, searched frantically for his father. He finally found him, calmly watching the fire, his face glowing in the reflection, his white hair blowing in the wind.

"My heart ached for him," said Charles. "He was 67 — no longer a young man — and everything was going up in flames. When he saw me, he shouted, 'Charles, where's your mother?' When I told him I didn't know, he said, 'Find her. Bring her here. She will never see anything like this as long as she lives.'"

The next morning, Edison looked at the ruins and said, "There is great value in disaster. All our mistakes are burned up. Thank God we can start anew."

Three weeks after the fire, Edison managed to deliver the first phonograph.

FAILURE OFTEN RESULTS FROM following the line of least persistence.

Despite the claims of book titles, magazine articles and assorted self-help gurus, there are no quick and easy ways to health, happiness, wealth, teamwork, or success. Most "overnight successes" take years to achieve. Most "natural talent" is created through thousands of hours of disciplined training and practice. (Indeed, the final level of mastery consists in making it look natural.) There are no "success secrets." However, there are success systems, success habits, and success principles — and these are applied through discipline and persistence.

As the 19th-century English biologist Thomas Henry Huxley once advised his students in a university address on medical education, "Patience and tenacity of purpose are worth more than twice their weight of cleverness."

We often think that successful people are those lucky enough to have won the "gene pool." They picked good parents and were born with great talent, intelligence, or other natural gifts. But we all know people with talent, perhaps even bordering on genius, who never did much with their abilities.

Many people give up just as they're about to achieve success. They often stop digging when they're inches from their vein of gold. Then they decide to prospect for silver, start digging in new places, get discouraged and give up just before they're about to reach their dreams.

Studies have shown that Nobel Prize winners most often have only average levels of intelligence compared to their peers, but exceptionally high levels of tenacity and persistence. They doggedly pursue their research or investigate theories long-abandoned by their less persistent colleagues.

Terry Fox, having lost his leg to cancer, embarked on a cross-Canada run called the "Marathon of Hope" to raise money for cancer research. With an artificial right leg, his shuffle-and-hop running style enabled him to cover about 24 miles per day.

Many people train for months and make a big deal out of running in a single marathon (26 miles). Terry ran close to a marathon a day — with an artificial leg!

He managed to run for 143 days and cover 3,339 miles — from St. John's, Newfoundland to Thunder Bay, Ontario — before cancer was discovered in his lungs and he was forced to abandon his run. A few months later he died. His inspiring legacy continues to this day in annual Terry Fox runs that have raised tens of millions of dollars for cancer research.

When asked how he kept himself going out there as exhaustion set in and he had thousands of miles ahead of him, he replied, "I just keep running to the next telephone pole."

THE FRENCH-BORN AMERICAN surgeon and biologist Alexis Carrel won a Nobel Prize for his work on vascular ligature and grafting of blood vessels and organs. His research experience led him to conclude that "life leaps like a geyser for those who drill through the rock of inertia."

We aren't losers until we quit trying. As the Japanese proverb teaches, the eventual winners are those who "fall down seven times, get up eight."

FACING A JOURNEY OF a thousand miles or the prospect of many years of effort can be discouraging. One way to deal with such daunting challenges is to break them into small, manageable pieces. It's like eating the proverbial elephant one bite at a time. (Not that I can imagine anyone wanting to eat an elephant; I often wonder about the sadists who come up with these expressions — skinning cats, boiling frogs, etc.)

Leaders make a habit of doing difficult tasks that most people avoid.

Deep discipline

The bedrock of character is self-discipline; the virtuous life, as philosophers since Aristotle have observed, is based on self-control. A related keystone of character is being able to motivate and guide oneself, whether in doing homework, finishing a job, or getting up in the morning. And, as we have seen, the ability to defer gratification and to control and channel one's urges to act is a basic emotional skill, one that in a former day was called will.

Daniel Goleman, *Emotional Intelligence: Why It Can Matter More Than IQ*

During the 1960s, psychologist Walter Mischel conducted what became known as "the marshmallow test" with four-year-olds in the preschool at Stanford University. The object of the exercise was to assess each preschooler's ability to delay gratification. Each child was given one marshmallow. They were told that they could eat it immediately or, if they waited until the researcher returned in 20 minutes, they could have two marshmallows.

Some kids in the group just couldn't wait. They gobbled down the marshmallow immediately. The rest struggled hard to resist eating it. They covered their eyes, talked to themselves, sang, played games, even tried to go to sleep. The preschoolers who were able to wait were rewarded with two marshmallows when the researcher returned.

Twelve to fourteen years later the same kids were re-evaluated. The differences were astonishing. Those who had been able to control their impulses and delay gratification as four-year-olds were more effective socially and personally as teenagers. They had higher levels of assertiveness, self-confidence, trustworthiness, dependability, and a superior ability to control stress. Remarkably, their Scholastic Aptitude Test (SAT) scores were also 210 points higher than the "instant gratification" group!

A KEY DIFFERENCE BETWEEN successful people — leaders — and those who struggle to get by is self-discipline. As Confucius wrote, "The nature of people is always the same; it is their habits that separate them." Successful people have formed the habits of doing those things that most people don't want to do.

Still, if discipline is a key to success, the fact is that most people would rather pick the lock. Less successful people can't pass up instant gratification in favor of some prospective benefit. It's much easier to live for the moment and let tomorrow take care of itself. But it takes discipline to forego the immediately pleasurable for an investment in the future.

In *The Road Less Traveled*, psychiatrist M. Scott Peck writes: "Delaying gratification is a process of scheduling the pain and pleasure of life in such a way as to enhance the pleasure by meeting and experiencing the pain first and getting it over with. It is the only decent way to live." He goes on to equate self-discipline with self-caring: "Discipline is the basic set of tools we require to solve life's problems. Without discipline we can solve nothing. With only some discipline we can solve only some problems. With total discipline we can solve all problems."

DISCIPLINE MEANS HAVING THE vision to see the long-term picture and keep things in balance. A Chinese proverb teaches that "if you are patient in one moment of anger, you will escape a hundred days of sorrow."

Regret can cost hundreds of hours, discipline costs minutes. An ounce of bite-my-tongue can outweigh a ton of I-am-so-sorries. One indication of our growth and maturity is what makes us angry — and how we express our anger. A boiling temper can really cook our goose.

We all want more patience. (And we want it now!) Most of us would like to be delivered from temptation, but we'd like it to stay in touch. Discipline is what keeps us going when the excitement of our first beginning a task is long past.

Former British prime minister Margaret Thatcher makes a key leadership point about discipline: "It's easy to be a starter, but are you a sticker, too? It's easy enough to begin a job. It's harder to see it through."

Discipline can be habit forming

Do every day or two something for no other reason than that you would rather not do it, so that when the hour of dire need draws nigh, it may find you not unnerved and untrained to stand the test.

William James, *Habit*

GOOD AND BAD HABITS are tiny daily choices that accumulate. Each choice is a small wire that is woven together with hundreds of other little choices. Eventually these wires form a strong cable.

Like a child that grows a tiny amount each day, our tiny choices accumulate without much notice. By the time we realize we have either a good or a bad habit, the habit has us.

Most of our daily choices are made automatically without even thinking about them. To change our habits, we first need to be aware of them. Then we need to work backward from the habit to the daily practices that form it. To change the habit, we need to change those practices.

Procrastination is a good example. Putting things off until tomorrow is a popular labor-saving device. However, as actor and comedian W.C. Fields once said, "There comes a time that you must take the bull by the tail and face the situation." Failing to face tough situations usually makes them worse. But it's a habit. The more often we procrastinate, the more natural it is to do the next time.

The opposite is also true. If we practice doing first all those things that we most want to delay, we find that those things aren't quite so bad as we imagined. And everything else that follows is all that much easier.

Our discipline and habits spring from our passion and commitment. I find that when I have the least amount of self-discipline and have the greatest trouble forming a success habit, it's often because my heart isn't in it. To motivate myself, then, I need to find ways to increase my passion.

For years I told myself how much I hated jogging early in the morning. I would clench my teeth and go for a short run because I knew it was good for me. I complained so much about jogging that my colleagues once bought me a T-shirt that featured a list of handy "running excuses."

Then I started to concentrate on all the benefits of jogging. I paid attention to the smells, sounds, and sights around me. I focused on how invigorated I felt in the shower afterward and how much more energy I had throughout the day. I talked about how much better I felt from the workout. I read articles on the benefits of aerobic exercise. I slowly extended my running distance.

Eventually I came to love jogging. When I broke my collar bone in a skiing accident (that's the time I discovered, painfully, the most dangerous statement on the ski hill: "Just follow me, Dad"), I went jogging with my shoulder bouncing painfully in an upper-body brace. Why? Some might say it was because I bumped my head too hard in the fall on the ski hill. I believe it's because the jogging habit had me.

PASSION IS A KEY element of leadership. In a *Fortune* article on "America's Most Admired Companies," Thomas A. Stewart gives direction that applies to every leader in any social, family, or organizational role. His advice also highlights one of the main reasons these leaders are so successful. "There is one more item in our list of Things Leaders Must Do, and it's just what your broker says Investors Must Not Do: fall in love. There are CEOs who slash and CEOs who fix and CEOs who safeguard and CEOs who build. The great ones do all these things too, but first of all they love. Passion, commitment, ferocity — the traits of lovers are in these leaders."

GROWING POINTS

- Too many people let their disappointments and cynicism slowly extinguish their life spark. On-the-job-retirees who waste their lives in a dead-end job they don't enjoy aren't making a living, they're making a dying.

- Leadership is the stuff of dreams, inspiration, excitement, desire, pride, care, passion, and love. This is the stuff of the heart, not the head. When we connect with our inner spirit, we feel the most intensely alive.

- Our work can just be a job or the canvas that allows us to paint a rich and textured portrait of our deeper selves. Meaningful work goes well beyond "what I do for a living"; it joyfully expresses what I do *with* my living.

- A burning commitment to the cause is a clear hallmark of passionate and highly effective leaders.

- Failure often results from following the line of least persistence. There are no "success secrets." However, there are success systems, success habits, and success principles applied through discipline and persistence.

- A key difference between successful people — leaders — and those who struggle to get by is self-discipline. Successful people have formed the habits of doing those things that most people don't want to do.

- Good and bad habits are tiny daily choices that accumulate. Each choice is a small wire that is woven together with hundreds of other little choices. Eventually these wires form a strong cable and the habit has us.

CHAPTER 6

WITH ALL MY HEART AND SOUL

What is the purpose of our work?
Of our lives? Material success alone is not
enough. Leaders seek within —
and find something more.

Spirit and Meaning

*Our responsibility as individuals is to be true to our own souls
and NOT sell out to the System. If we cannot help heal
the System we are in, then we must leave the System and find a better
opportunity, even if we have to create our own system to do it.*

Dorothy E. Fischer, "The System Versus the Soul,"
an essay in *Rediscovering the Soul of Business:
A Renaissance of Values*

Let's Be Frank (I): Running on Empty

Frank is a regional manager in a fast-growing technology company. Many major corporations in his area are clients and he's a trusted consultant to their senior executives. As the top producer in his firm, he's considered a key contributor to the company's incredible success.

Frank's a legendary "bottom line" guy. He not only "makes his numbers" (often by dramatically overshooting his targets) but is also an impressive strategist and problem solver. The crisp analysis and marketing smarts he displays during budget presentations and operational reviews are the envy of other managers.

With a career path leading to vice president and an above-average shot at eventually becoming CEO, Frank has a six-figure salary plus large performance bonuses, profit sharing, and stock options. He wears his success like the expensive designer suits that fill his walk-in closet. He drives luxury cars, lives in a beautiful home, and takes his family on exotic vacations. He has it all.

Yet recently, Frank has begun fantasizing about suicide.

"I've got to relieve the unbearable pressure," he keeps thinking. He is desperate to kill the gnawing emptiness that now comes with each new success. No matter how much he achieves, it's never enough. There's so much more to reach for and there's never enough time to do it all. The tension headaches are becoming more intense. Each day, the treadmill seems to be going a little bit faster. People are no longer human. Customers have become revenue streams — their importance measured in terms of their sales potential. Company employees are just another set of resources (these happen to have skin wrapped around them) to be driven to maximum production.

At a recent meeting to address the company's growing levels of internal dissatisfaction, the new president dismissed employee complaints as the product of "a wailing pack of whiners who will never be happy."

"We can't let their bitching and moaning distract us from our business results," the president declared. Frank nodded. The emptiness in his gut growled like hunger pangs.

Would this be his last meeting?

SPIRIT AND MEANING IS a missing link in many lives, communities, and organizations. They may enjoy material prosperity but live in spiritual poverty. That's what's driving the rapidly growing number of "meaning seekers" in our society. We want to know that our lives count for something. We want to make a difference. Our work and our lives become more meaningful when they are in harmony with who we are, and when they touch the very core of why we exist. We are spiritual beings having a human experience. Those times when we feel the most love, passion, or energy are the times we are most alive. That's when our soul sings.

In *Leading with Soul: An Uncommon Journey of Spirit*, organization consultants and professors Lee Bolman and Terrence Deal (co-author of the classic *Corporate Cultures* — the 1982 book that popularized the idea of organization culture) conclude, "The signs point toward spirit and soul as the essence of leadership."

The culture of a family, workgroup, or organization is often described as "the way we do things around here." A toxic culture is loveless, passionless, and meaningless. It has a weak heart and a sick soul. A healthy culture is engaged in meaningful *doing* through purposeful *being*. It has a high-energy spirit.

Leaders make work, families, communities — or life in general — purposeful. I can only do that if I am filled with purpose. Spirit and meaning start inside the leader. They can only be developed from the inside out.

If we live without soul, without love, and without meaning, we don't really live at all.

Dead Ends

> *A daydream is a meal at which images are eaten.*
> *Some of us are gourmets, some gourmands,*
> *and a good many take their images precooked out*
> *of a can and swallow them down whole,*
> *absent-mindedly and with little relish.*

W. H. Auden, *The Dyer's Hand*

Let's Be Frank (II): Hitting the Wall

One evening after an especially hectic day, Frank decided to join a few others from the office at their favorite "watering hole" around the corner. Sheila had asked him — as she had many times before — and she expected another "no, thanks. I've got too much going on today." But this time was different. Something told Frank he should go along this time.

Over the second round of drinks, the conversation turned toward the company's growing morale problems. Ruthless new competitors and massive changes in their industry were forcing everyone to scramble to keep up. The company's legendary growth rates were dropping off. The dreaded and previously unused "L word" — layoffs — was now whispered in the halls and lunchrooms.

Joan's voice broke with emotion as she talked about her growing health problems and the steep price her family has been paying for her "successful career." "Maybe it's time to find another job," Geoff dared to suggest.

"What, and give up the company's outstanding health and family benefits package?" Joan angrily retorted.

Escaping to the men's room, Frank felt the walls getting a little closer. The feeling of being trapped was back again. The emptiness pangs chewed at his stomach so hard he felt like he was going to throw up. In one of the toilet stalls someone had scrawled, "Death is nature's way of telling you to slow down."

It was, Frank knew, time to take action.

PSYCHOLOGIST ABRAHAM MASLOW DEVELOPED a hierarchy describing our progression from the most basic needs to the highest need of self-actualization — the fulfillment of our full potential. He believed that "the unhappiness, unease and unrest in the world today are caused by people living far below their capacity."

In his book, *The Greatest Miracle in the World*, Og Mandino spins a tale of his encounters with Simon Potter, a humble and learned wise man. In one conversation, Og and Simon discuss the miracle people can perform in their own lives by resurrecting their dead spirits. Simon explains the need for this miracle: "Most humans, in varying degrees, are already dead. In one way or another they have lost their dreams, their ambitions, their desire for a better life. They have surrendered their fight for self-esteem and they have compromised their great potential. They have settled for a life of mediocrity, days of despair and nights of tears. They are no more than living deaths confined to cemeteries of their choice."

We need to be less afraid of death and more frightened by an empty life.

In their "big busyness," organizations can easily lose their heart and soul. Without realizing it, or ever intending to, they can lose their deeper sense of meaning. Goals, plans, reports, and numbers take over. In the harsh glare of hard-headed analysis, soft "touchy feely" emotions like spirit and meaning evaporate as dew in the morning sun. It's like an academic study of a deeply moving story. The dissection may help us understand the technical aspects of the composition, but misses the feelings that touched us so deeply.

Regardless of our positions in an organization, we need to do whatever we can to help change that. We need to be part of the solution, not part of the problem. But we need to ensure we're not feeling like victims of a heartless team or organization with a hollowed-out soul. It's too easy to find ourselves being numbed by jobs that aren't a passionate joy, but really feel like work.

Profit, wealth, or careers can become goals in themselves rather than the means to fulfilling our deeper, more meaningful destinies. If we're not in touch with our hearts and souls, we may not realize how our life energy is being slowly drained by work that doesn't feed our spirit and give us richer meaning. If we're not careful, we can become hollow victims, our lifeblood sucked out of us.

If we don't see a point in our lives and work, the need for change is equally meaningless.

In Search of Meaning

What is the meaning of human life, or for that matter of the life of any creature? You ask: Does it make any sense to pose this question? I answer: The man who regards his own life and that of his fellow creatures as meaningless is not merely unhappy but hardly fit for life.

Albert Einstein

Let's Be Frank (III): Trying to Fill the Void

With his typical intensity, Frank began searching for ways to deal with his emptiness. He checked out a few churches and attended introductory classes for various inner-development and spiritual groups. He started reading books on spirituality, soul, and personal growth.

One day he came across a passage in an old report that really spoke to him. It seemed like the authors were reaching back across the decades to shine a big we-told-you-this-would-be-the-result spotlight on his life. Reading the report, written in 1958 as part of the Rockefeller Report on Education, Frank felt like he was a victim of society's failure to act on the warnings the authors sounded so many years ago:

"What most people want — young or old — is not merely security, or comfort, or luxury, although they are glad enough to have these. Most of all they want meaning in their lives. If our era and our culture and our leaders do not, or cannot, offer great meanings, great objectives, great convictions, then people will settle for shallow and trivial substitutes. This is a deficiency for which we all bear a responsibility…. This is the challenge of our times."

They didn't solve it then and it's worse now, Frank mused. Why continue suffering?

ONE OF THE BIGGEST social movements of our time is society's search for meaning. Books on spirituality, soul, and personal growth are continually popping up on bestseller lists. The Internet is filling with similarly themed sites and discussion groups. Numerous surveys show that the vast majority of people in almost every society in the world believe in some higher power. Conferences on spirituality in the workplace and soulful leadership have become regular events attracting thousands of "meaning seekers."

Without a deeper sense of meaning, change and the hectic pace of life can be overwhelming and unconnected. People we're trying to lead or help change may see the need for many changes and even understand why they're necessary. But unless the change really connects with their deeper being — their heart and soul — they will just go along....for now.

In his book, *Going Deep: Exploring Spirituality in Life and Leadership*, psychologist Ian Percy outlines a very useful change or development framework — the "PIES" model, which helps to chart the depth of commitment to a personal, family, team, or organizational change. The depth of the commitment shows how likely the change is really make a lasting difference.

The first and most superficial level is Political. At this level appearances are everything. We make a "politically correct" change and try to show that we will "get with the program." The next level of depth is Intellectual. Here's where a good business case or logical argument wins the day. Facts and analysis convince us that the change makes sense. Both of these first two levels deal with the head.

At the third level, Emotional, we're dealing with the heart. The change feels right. We want to make it happen because it excites us. The fourth, and deepest, level of commitment is Spiritual. We make the change because it is in step with our deeper selves. The direction of the family, group, or organization and its underlying purpose touches our very soul. At this level, Percy explains, "There is no gap and no separation between belief and action. The gap has been filled by the very essence of who you are. You and the object of your commitment have become one."

In what is too often a mad dash from cradle to grave, we need to take time — in work and life — to nourish our inner selves.

True to our Souls

> *Everyone has a special purpose, a special talent or gift to give to others, and it is your duty to discover what it is. Your special talent is God's gift to you. What you do with your talent is your gift to God.*

Gautama Chopra, *Child of the Dawn: A Magical Journey of Awakening*

Let's Be Frank (IV): A Path to Follow

As he struggled to deal with what he was now calling his "trapped emptiness," Frank came across a poem on the Internet entitled "The Dash." It was written by a former football player and student of Lou Holtz. Frank discovered that the legendary Notre Dame football coach closes many of his speaking engagements by reading this poem. At the heart of the poem are four lines that really jumped out at Frank:

I've seen my share of tombstones but never took the time to truly read

The meaning behind what is there for others to see

Under the person's name it read the date of birth, dash, and the date the person passed

But the more I think about the tombstone, the important thing is the dash.

Thinking about his own "dash" gave Frank a path to follow in his search for meaning. I didn't choose my date of birth, and unless I take things into my own hands, I won't get to choose the day I die, Frank reflected. But how I live now is completely up to me. It's my responsibility. It's my choice. What really matters most to me? he asked himself. What will my dash eventually be remembered for? What's my legacy to be? Who will care?

THE AMERICAN PHILOSOPHER AND poet George Santayana once said, "There is no cure for birth and death save to enjoy the interval."

For many years I helped coach our son Chris's baseball team. One warm June evening we were driving home from a game. We had the windows down and sunroof open as we listened to the world's greatest baseball team — the Toronto Blue Jays(!) — beating up the Yankees again.

Chris seemed to be off in another world. Suddenly he turned to me with wonderment in his voice and said, "Dad, do you ever have those seconds when it just clicks in your head that everything is perfect?" I thought for a minute and then replied, "Not as often as I used to. I've become too busy reaching for the future to enjoy the moment."

LIFE IS A TIME-LIMITED offer. Too often our "dash" becomes a mad dash. We rush around trying to do and have it all. We become human doings rather than human beings. We provide for our bodily needs while starving our souls. We lose sight of what really matters. We become truer to our ego than our soul.

Artist, writers, and performers often talk about "finding their voice." Their art becomes an expression of their inner selves. The people with the deepest and most meaningful lives are those who have found and use their inner voice. Their life sings from their soul.

The ancient Roman poet Horace poses a core-being question: "Why do you hasten to remove anything which hurts your eye, while if something affects your soul you postpone the cure until next year?"

OUR WORK IS A way that we can be true to our souls. Toward the end of his life, impressionist painter Auguste Renoir had severe arthritis in his hands. But his inner voice was not easily silenced. To continue expressing himself through his painting, he had his brushes strapped to his wrists. A friend asked why he imposed such pain and inconvenience upon himself. Without hesitation, Renoir answered, "The pain is momentary, but the art will last."

Regardless of how humble or prestigious society may consider what we do, our work should be a key means of finding and expressing our voice. In a Labor Day speech given just after the turn of the 20th century, U.S. president Theodore Roosevelt declared, "Far and away the best prize that life offers is the chance to work hard at work worth doing."

Our work is part of our dash. If it's just a job that I do half-heartedly and half-well, I make myself miserable and starve my soul. My inner voice develops laryngitis if I am in a job I hate (or just tolerate) and don't take pride in the quality of what I do.

When our work is part of a deeper life calling, we put our heart into it. Our work becomes our contribution to making this team, this organization, and this world just a little better because we passed this way. That's when what we do becomes a meaningful expression of who we are.

Leaders share a love that is expressed in a deep desire to see their family members, co-workers, and organizations grow to their full potential.

The Many Faces of Love

> *A human being is part of a whole, called by us the Universe, a part limited in time and space. He experiences himself, his thoughts and feelings, as something separated from the rest — a kind of optical delusion of his consciousness. This delusion is a kind of prison for us, restricting us to our personal desires and to affection for a few persons nearest us. Our task must be to free ourselves from this prison by widening our circles of compassion to embrace all living creatures and the whole of nature in its beauty.*

Albert Einstein

Let's Be Frank (V): Seeing the Light

The pinkish orange glow of the rising sun bathed the oak-paneled study in a warm light unlike any Frank had ever experienced. It pulsed with life. As the shimmering hues embraced him, Frank felt like his body dissolved into millions of pieces that floated throughout the room, dancing with the light. He felt bursts of energy and insights that he hadn't felt for years. The room seemed to expand forever. Slowly his body seemed to materialize and return to his chair. Then that empty vacuum in his gut popped open and was flooded with the magical light.

During the past few months, Frank had started the habit of rising before dawn for study and attempts at meditation (he could never quite still his racing mind). As the latest in a string of such books, this morning he was continuing with M. Scott Peck's classic *The Road Less Traveled: A New Psychology of Love, Traditional Values and Spiritual Growth*. He underlined a key passage, "I define love thus: The will to extend one's self for the purpose of nurturing one's own or another's spiritual growth."

"What a strange way to think about love," Frank thought. He had always experienced love as a warm friendship, special closeness, burning passion, or sexual desire. He read on: "Since I am human and you are human, to love humans means to love myself as well as you. To be dedicated to human spiritual development is to be dedicated to the race of which we are a part, and this therefore means dedication to our own development as well as 'theirs.'"

Reflecting on the passage he had read, Frank let the book slide to the floor as he stared out the window and let his thoughts swirl around him. That's when the light show started.

He once thought he loved his wife Debbie. They had been married 12 years. Their oldest was eight-year-old Rachel. Four-year-old Joel was the baby of the family. The first real conversation Deb and Frank had had in months was last week when she laid down terms for their separation. Life just got so busy and they had drifted apart into their own separate, lonely lives.

During their discussion, Deb told Frank about a couple they'd known for years whose marriage suddenly broke up. The husband just packed up and left home one night. Deb quipped that it would be six weeks before she'd notice if Frank did the same thing. The straw that broke the back of their marriage was Deb's growing suspicion of Frank's office affair with Michelle. But Deb could never pin it down because Frank was so quick on his feet with believable explanations. She told Frank that the best revenge she could think of for Michelle was to let her have him.

Looking at love as extending yourself for your own or other's spiritual growth, Frank realized he didn't really love Deb or the kids. What he thought was love for Michelle, was really lust. In that morning's flash of light and insight, Frank suddenly knew that he couldn't love others because he didn't love himself. He didn't care about the growth and development of anyone else because his inner growth and development had stalled. His highly admired drive for success and status was an escape. He tried to overcome his inner emptiness by filling his life with outer busyness. It was time for change.

LIKE LEADERSHIP, LOVE HAS many faces and forms. Both are states of being that defy easy definitions or how-to formulas. Pianist Arthur Rubinstein describes one face of love: "I'm passionately involved in life: I love its change, its color, its movement. To be alive, to be able to see, to walk, to have houses, music, paintings — it's all a miracle."

Author and lecturer Leo Buscaglia outlines another face of love when talking about a contest he was asked to judge. The purpose of the contest was to find the most caring child. The winner was a four-year-old whose next-door neighbor was an elderly gentleman who had recently lost his wife. Upon seeing the man cry, the little boy went into the old gentleman's yard, climbed onto his lap, and just sat there. When his mother asked him what he had said to the neighbor, the little boy said, "Nothing, I just helped him cry."

Highly effective leaders are in love with the organization, community, or team in which they work or live. Their love is expressed in a deep desire to see that organization, community, or team grow to its full potential. Leaders love the people they work with enough to contribute to their growth and development.

That doesn't mean we always like or agree with everyone. As with relatives, we often don't get to pick and choose neighbors, teammates, bosses, and the like. Some of them aren't people we'd invite to dinner or choose as a friend. However, leaders love their organization's greater purpose and see its products or services contributing to a bigger world that they love. That love — and desire for growth and development — extends to everyone involved.

Starting with ourselves

LOVE OF OTHERS STARTS with love of self. The desire to see others grow and develop starts with our own personal growth and development. If we're not leading a meaningful life, it's hard to help others find meaning. If we don't feel a sense of connection to a bigger purpose or being, it's hard to unify others. Spirit and meaning are an inside job. Inner growth is part of our spiritual renewal process. Our soul craves it.

Since the beginning of civilization, humans have pursued growth. We've restlessly tried to do and have more and more. For most of the history of the western world, growth has been expressed in the outer, material world — possessions, territory, money, economies, etc. But now our environmental awareness and shifting values are showing us some of the limits to outer, material growth.

We are now moving to a stage of inner, spiritual growth. This is new territory. But like those who were part of the industrial revolution, we are just getting an inkling of the awesome power and exciting new world that the Inner Revolution will open up for us in the next few decades.

Centered leaders are continually exploring inner space. They draw outward leadership strength from their heart and soul.

Living Inside Out

> *By changing our beliefs, our perceptions, we cause our experience to change, and in this way we change the world around us. There is no true boundary or limit to the self; there is no separation from the world that encircles us. When we master the forces within, we influence the forces without.*

Gautama Chopra, *Child of the Dawn: A Magical Journey of Awakening*

Let's Be Frank (VI): Finding the Voice Within

Frank decided to quit his job. The price of "success" was too high. The awakening he experienced that morning in his study helped him realize that he needed to get off the speeding treadmill before he killed himself. But what did he really want? Frank had spent most of his adult life chasing society's definition of success. What was his? What did he value most? Where would he ideally like to be? What was his purpose or reason for being?

Frank spent weeks wrestling with these questions. He started keeping a personal journal to record his thoughts and feelings. He hoped this might help him learn more about himself and understand what really mattered most to him. He realized that his values had become centered around wealth, career success, and personal recognition.

After thinking hard about what values he wanted to build his life around, Frank finally identified his real priorities: family, continuous personal growth, financial security, and a job that connected with his soul. Identifying a personal purpose or reason for being was especially tough. But after a while, the elusive answer came. As Frank wrote in his journal, "I am here to learn how to grow personally and enrich my inner life. I will try to help others do the same. I will contribute to society by raising children who become effective adults, doing meaningful work that makes a difference, and strengthening my community and country."

Frank's vision of his preferred future began to take shape as well. He'd always enjoyed literature and live theater (but in recent years had no time to enjoy either). He began to dream about moving to a small town famous for its theater and summer festivals. Knowing how the town and theater was struggling, he saw himself using his considerable marketing talent to help revive the struggling community. He took a few trips to the town to look at houses and investigate the possibilities.

There still remained the issue of Frank's marriage, which was in big trouble. The first step was to admit his affair to Deb and break off the relationship with Michelle. Understandably, Deb remained angry and hurt. They began seeing a therapist for marriage counseling. But it didn't seem to do much to bridge the huge rift between them.

In one of the growing number of painful discussions about their future, it dawned on Frank that he and Deb had spent more time planning their vacations and buying cars and homes than they'd spent planning their lives together. So he suggested they try establishing a joint vision of their ideal future together, clarify their key values, and try to write a statement of purpose.

Frank started by sharing his recently acquired idea of moving to the small theater town. Deb listened patiently. When he was finished, she sat in icy silence. Finally she exploded, "Your postcard picture of artsy theater and small-town life is unbelievably selfish! Did it ever occur to you that I don't want to drop my career and leave my friends here? What about the kids? Do you really think they want to be uprooted so you can play the hero — the big man about town?"

Frank responded in kind. He could give as much fire and venom as he ever got from anyone else. But in his heart, he knew she was right. A few days later, when they'd both cooled off, Frank and Deb took another stab at developing a joint picture of their ideal future together.

It was tough work. Many of the pent-up frustrations and issues they should have dealt with long ago finally gushed out. At times they had to break off discussions and go their separate ways. But as the weeks passed, a picture of their possible shared future took shape. The question now was, could they rebuild their relationship and bridge the huge gaps that had grown between them?

THINK ABOUT A FEW special people you know personally who are strong leaders. They may be a manager, team member, teacher, family member, or community leaders. Chances are that one of their special characteristics is their strong sense of self.

Leaders know who they are (or aren't), where they want to go, and what really matters most. They care about the opinions of others, but they don't try to please everybody and meekly play the parts that others want them to play. As authentic leaders, they don't lead their lives from the outside in. Rather, they lead from the inside out.

Inside-out leadership comes from deep within. It is leading from our center. Centered leaders are continually exploring inner space and drawing outer leadership strength from their heart and soul. This is how they enrich their lives. It is the source of the spirit and meaning they bring to their families, teams, or organizations.

The challenge — even the obligation — of leadership is to help others care about who they are and what they do.

Take My Meaning

An essential factor in leadership is the ability to influence and organize meaning.

Warren Bennis and Joan Goldsmith, *Learning to Lead*

Let's Be Frank (VII): Reaching the Other Side

Frank had broken through his "trapped emptiness." He had a renewed sense of hope and purpose. He was energized. Life was worth living.

Frank understood, too, that the greener grass on the other side of the fence often turns out to be astroturf. He realized that quitting his job and moving to that small festival theater town was just an escape. Deb and the kids were quite happy to stay put. As Deb said one night, "We could move to another house or take other jobs, but our problems would hitch themselves to the moving van and move in with us."

With a lot of additional work and trust building, they just might be able to save their marriage. They both agreed it was worth the effort.

Frank also came to realize how much he loved and believed in the products and services his company provided. They were making a difference to the lives of thousands of people.

If the company didn't keep quality and service levels high, planes and computer systems could crash. Hospital operating rooms could go dark. Cars could malfunction. Factories could lose production and become less efficient. Somehow everyone had lost sight of that.

The focus was on immediate measures such as daily production, sales volumes, cost containment, and budgets. All of which was necessary, of course, but it didn't go deep enough. A budget doesn't tug at the heart strings

(although missing budget targets can cause some managers to rip hearts out). Business plans don't touch the soul.

Frank knew that only people connecting with people can provide that deep and satisfying sense of meaning. He worked hard to help his team reconnect with the sense of purpose and meaning that Frank now felt. They focused on customers and what impact the organization's products and services were having on their lives. He encouraged personal calls and visits to customers. He brought customers into meetings and planning sessions to discuss how they were using the company's products and services.

WHAT CAN WE TAKE away from Frank's story? Once he connected with his deeper self, he reconnected the people in his organization with their vision, values, and purpose. He continually referred back to them during meetings and planning sessions. He built appreciation, recognition, and celebrations around them. He linked hiring and promotions to them. He even helped the company expand their leadership development programs to include role descriptions, personal feedback, and coaching on how to strengthen spirit and meaning. Frank still has a long way to go yet, but he is starting to reconnect everyone's heart and soul. The joy of work and life is breaking through the clouds.

In my consulting firm, we often bring groups of people together to get their perspectives on strengths and weaknesses, improvement opportunities, and the like. One morning I asked a group of very quiet production and service people a series of these questions. I was getting very few responses. This was going nowhere fast. Finally one grizzled veteran sitting at the back of the room with his arms folded said, "Jim, I think you're confusing us with people who care."

Assuming we care — and if we don't, we're in the wrong place — the leadership challenge (even obligation) is to help others care. In today's environment, this is one of the toughest aspects of leadership. Partially that's a symptom of the widespread Victimitis Virus — the hopelessness and powerlessness of poor-little-me syndrome.

Cynicism is also running wild, as popular cartoon strips (and associated books) show nothing but the negative sides of organizational life, and paint all managers as bumbling idiots. Whole cultures can become infected with this lack of meaning and emptiness.

Downsizing and layoffs have also reduced loyalties and commitment. If we can't help others become ever more committed to the organization, we can help them increase their commitment to the organization's cause. This involves aligning the personal purpose and values of people with the team or organization's deeper reason for being.

At my firm, we try to express this essential leadership element through the following values statement:

We're here to make the world a better place. Our overarching purpose is to make a difference in each other's lives and in the lives of those we serve. We maintain a healthy bottom line to provide financial strength and stability, but money isn't our primary focus. We know that if we serve our customers well and manage our business effectively, profits will be our reward.

QUEEN BEES GIVE OFF a chemical substance that keeps the hive together. It has been called "the spirit of the hive." Few of us can sit around strictly as queen bees — although it is a tempting thought. We need to be worker bees as well.

It's a balance issue: As we contribute our work to our team or organization, we also need to contribute a sense of meaning or purpose. Regardless of our formal role, we need to help build the spirit of the team. This leadership comes from our own center. I can only contribute the spirit and meaning that I feel. I need to lead with all my heart and soul.

GROWING POINTS

- One of the biggest social movements of our time is society's search for meaning. We want to know that our lives count for something. We want to make a difference.

- A toxic culture is loveless, passionless, and meaningless. It has a weak heart and a sick soul. A healthy culture is engaged in meaningful doing through purposeful being. It has a high-energy spirit.

- Life is a time-limited offer. Too often our "dash" becomes a mad dash. Our work is part of our dash. When our work is part of a deeper life calling, we put our heart into it. That's when what we do becomes a meaningful expression of who we are.

- Leaders love their organization's greater purpose and see its products or services contributing to a bigger world that they love. That love — and desire for growth and development — extends to everyone involved.

- Centered leaders are continually exploring inner space and drawing outer leadership strength from their heart and soul. It is the source of the spirit and meaning they bring to their families, teams, or organizations.

- Assuming we care (if not, we're in the wrong place), the leadership challenge is to help others care. We need to help build the spirit of the team or organization.

CHAPTER 7

FROM PHASE OF LIFE TO WAY OF LIFE

What's our best defence against being victims of change? To grow and develop every day; to change ourselves — and to lead others in the process.

Growing and Developing

The fatal metaphor of progress, which means leaving things behind us, has utterly obscured the real idea of growth, which means leaving things inside us.·

G. K. Chesterton, *Fancies Versus Fads*

Marti was driving through her neighborhood to work one morning when a genie suddenly appeared in the passenger seat and asked, "And what will your third wish be?"

Marti was so startled, she almost hit a lamp post. After pulling over to the curb and stopping the car, she glared angrily at the genie and practically shouted, "How can I be getting a third wish when I haven't had a first or second wish yet?"

"You have had two wishes already," the genie calmly replied, "but your second wish was for me to put everything back the way it was before you made your first wish. So you remember nothing, because everything is the way it was before you made any wishes. You have one wish left."

Already late for work, Marti thought about her hectic life and blurted, "Okay, I don't believe this, but why not; I wish my world would slow down and stop moving so fast. I wish we lived on easy street. I wish there was more stability and security at work, at home, and here in our community. I wish life was more predictable and things didn't keep changing."

"Funny," said the genie as it granted Marti's wish and disappeared forever. "That was your first wish, too."

WE DO NEED TO be careful about what we wish for — we just might get it. The popular goals of security, stability, and predictability are deadly. The closer we get to these dangerous goals, the more our growth is stunted and learning reduced. In today's fast-changing world, if we fail to change, it is we who will be changed.

Take the notion of "job security," for example. Sure, it sounds attractive, but it can draw us into the poisonous swamps of rot and decay. The more secure I become in my job, the more likely I am to become stagnant, stuck in a rut. A high level of job security means I feel less and less urgency to grow, develop, and build new skills.

Remember, change is inevitable. And eventually that change will affect *everyone's* job, leaving those who are unprepared as victims. Ironically, it is "job security" that most often leads us down the slippery slope to a future with very little security indeed.

True and lasting security comes from constant growth and development. We can't manage change, but we can be change *opportunists*. The higher our rate of personal growth and development, the more likely we are to master the opportunities that change unexpectedly throws in front of us. To master change and build a life of ever-deeper growth, we need to make learning a way of life rather than a phase of life.

LEADERS ARE CONSTANTLY ON the grow. Much as in financial planning, where one of the key principles is to "pay yourself first," highly effective leaders devote *at least* 10% of their time to personal growth and development.

The first step in achieving growth and development is having *the desire* to do so. Many people (and organizations) seem to think they can skip this step. They want to harvest the benefits of growth and development without planting the seeds of a personal growth plan, then fertilizing it with strong learning habits.

Ultimately, it is from their own growth and development that leaders help (or lead) others in growing and developing. This is a function of skills (doing) and values (being). The more we value (love) others, the more we care about their growth and development.

But we can't make others into something that we are not ourselves. Parents with stunted personal growth have a tough time raising their kids to learn, develop, and grow — just as, in the workplace, growth-deficient managers or group leaders aren't likely to develop learning and growing teams or organizations. Developing them means developing me.

There's nothing more dangerous than a comfortable rut.

Slow Death

The most fatal illusion is the settled point of view. Since life is growth and motion, a fixed point of view kills anybody who has one.

Brooks Atkinson, Pulitzer Prize-winning journalist

sidor Isaac Rabi was an Austrian-born American physicist who won a Nobel Prize in physics for his work in nuclear science. He was once asked how he became a scientist. Rabi explained that each day after school his mother would discuss his school day with him. She was less interested in what he had learned than in whether he "asked a good question today." She encouraged inquiry and curiosity in all that young Isidor did. "Asking good questions," Rabi explained, "made me become a scientist."

LIKE ISIDOR RABI, MANY people experience considerable growth during their days at school. But when their formal education comes to an end, so, too, does the questioning that leads to growth development.

When we see learning as a *phase* of life rather than a *way* of life, it's easy to become set in our point of view. As our personal growth rate slows and time goes by, we can become one of those know-it-all boors (and we've all suffered their company) who have many answers and few questions. Approaching middle age, we can end up with our broad mind trading places with our narrow waist. We can become so narrow-minded that we have to stack our ideas vertically.

THERE'S A WORLD OF DIFFERENCE between growing with age and simply growing old. With age can come wisdom, but too often age comes alone. Age to the stagnant is winter; but to a leader on the grow, it is harvest time.

Not all experience is equal. Experience isn't what happens to us, it's what we *do with* what happens to us. There's a major difference between growth experience and stagnation experience. Maybe we've shown up for work year after year and put in the time, but that doesn't mean we've gained by the experience. We may just be going through the motions, like taking the same route day after day; soon we're numbed to the passing landscape. We're in a rut.

Personal growth, continuous improvement, life-long learning… these are mantras for many people today. But good intentions often don't translate into action. It isn't always easy to recognize when we've slipped into the stagnant waters of stability and certainty. Like putting on weight, it happens gradually — until one day we notice how out of shape we've become.

Consider the following signs of stagnation and see if they sound familiar.

- *We've always done it that way*. We don't challenge our assumptions and reflect frequently on how we should do things now.

- *I am too old to change*. In Vincent Barry's *The Dog Ate My Homework*, this learning cop-out is described as "some senior's socially sanctioned refusal to acknowledge and take responsibility for attitudes, actions, and circumstances well within his or her power to influence." He goes on to write: "It's also about dying before one's time by living halfheartedly the time one has left. In this respect, 'I'm too old to change' is about all of us who refuse to live by refusing to change; for 'to change is to mature, [and] to mature is to go on creating oneself endlessly.'"

- *Losing our childlike curiosity*. Our sense of wonder and discovery is replaced with cynicism and apathy, often expressed as "been there, done that, what else is new." Pablo Picasso, one of the most prolific painters in history (with more than 20,000 works), once observed that "every child is an artist. The problem is how to remain an artist once he grows up."

- *Learning strictly through our own experience.* It's often better to borrow the experiences of others than to learn merely from our own. This can be not only less painful, but a much faster method of learning. Resources such as books, seminars, mentoring, networking, and group problem solving are just some of the things we can use to learn from other people's experience.

- *Being a creature of habit.* It's very easy to slip into routines that close us off from new approaches and learning. Our thinking can fall victim to repeated clichés, platitudes, and dogma. In *The Tragic Sense of Life*, Spanish philosopher Miguel de Unamuno writes, "To fall into habit is to begin to cease to be."

- *Having all the answers.* Writing in his personal journal in 1852, French artist Eugène Delacroix noted that "mediocre people have an answer for everything and are astonished at nothing. They always want to have the air of knowing better than you what you are going to tell them.... a capable and superior look is the natural accompaniment of this type of character."

- *Being complacently satisfied.* Only a mediocre person is always at his or her best. If I am getting very comfortable with my expertise and skill levels, my learning has leveled out. I am not stretching and challenging myself enough. My comfort zone is fossilizing into a complacency zone.

- *Fearing to attempt.* We know that the turtle only makes progress by sticking his head out. Yet we sit and dream about what we're going to do — some-day. If we don't take steady steps toward our dreams, the walls around our complacency zone get ever higher and thicker.

- *Having a fuzzy focus.* Our growth and development should be taking us somewhere. If we don't know where we want to go, what we stand for, or why we're here, any experience and learning path will do. We just wander around and hope for the best.

We can just manage change as it hits us. Or we can prepare for it through an ongoing process of discovery.

Always on the Grow

In a time of drastic change it is the learners who inherit the future. The learned usually find themselves equipped to live in a world that no longer exists.

Eric Hoffer, *Reflections on the Human Condition*

Hank had all the answers. He was a legend in his own mind. A very experienced and knowledgeable senior technician, people were constantly drawing on his analytical abilities. There didn't seem to be a technical or system problem he couldn't solve. Hank had little patience for the less-informed, however, and he used his technical know-how like a sword to "cut down the fools" who didn't follow his flawless logic. If he wanted any bright ideas, he'd give them to you.

Since turbulence was buffeting the company from many sides at once, various change and improvement efforts were underway. These included focusing on customer needs and improving service levels, cross-departmental teams, process improvements, leadership development, and an enterprise-wide integration of computer systems.

Hank dismissed most of the company's efforts with his usual cynicism. "If we lay low long enough, this too shall pass," he liked to quip. "I've been round and round the mulberry bush on this before. So many of these management fads are like the ties in my closet; if I wait long enough, they'll come back in fashion."

Gillian was a very knowledgeable senior technician who worked alongside Hank. They were about the same age and had both started in the company around the same time. She had a lot of respect for Hank's quick intellect, had learned a lot from him, and continued to draw from his technical expertise.

But Gillian's approach to problem solving relied less on dispensing quick answers than on initiating a process of asking questions. She was constantly asking why — and digging deeper to understand the underlying technical,

process, or human issues involved. She seemed to have an insatiable curiosity about a wide variety of subjects, both on and off the job. She was constantly reading, surfing the Internet, taking a course, or networking with colleagues in other companies.

Gillian's motto was summed up in a Henry Ford quotation she'd framed and put on her desk: "Anyone who stops learning is old, whether at twenty or eighty. Anyone who keeps learning stays young. The greatest thing in life is to keep your mind young." She supported the company's floundering change and improvement initiatives because she knew how critical they were to meeting the changes hitting their industry.

Ivano was Hank and Gillian's manager, and he had a troubling decision to make. As part of the company's major organizational changes, he and his vice president had agreed that the department needed to be restructured and reduced in size. There wasn't going to be room for both Hank and Gillian.

"We've struggled with our change programs because they've been just that — programs, rather than a way of life," the vice president said. "We've got to go deeper. We have to shift our culture toward continuous learning and constant improvement. We need to build a focused, fast, and flexible department around the remaining senior technician." No discussion was needed as to who that person would be; they both agreed that Gillian was the obvious choice.

Ivano dreaded the scene he would have with Hank. He also felt sorry for him. With his rigid mind-set, poor people skills, and traditional view of the world, Hank would have a tough time finding another job.

GILLIAN DEMONSTRATED — and Hank discovered too late — that what I am going to be tomorrow is determined by what I am becoming today. If I continue to do what I've always been doing, I will continue to get what I've always been getting. To get somewhere else, I need to grow into someone else.

If I have a clear picture of my preferred future and I am growing and developing toward that, the odds of my getting there rise dramatically. If I am a couch potato, I probably won't get much further in life than my couch. If I am a "mouse potato" (Internet widows/widowers will understand this term), I can be wasting my on-line computer time or wisely investing it. Growth or rot are the direct results, respectively, of the learning habits or the stagnation that flow from our choices.

The famed ancient Greek mathematician Euclid was hired to teach geometry to a young, impatient Egyptian heir to the throne. The prince was an unmotivated student. He especially resisted learning basic formulas and theories before getting into practical applications.

"Is there no simpler way you can get to the point?" he asked. "As the crown prince I should not be expected to deal with such trivial and useless details."

Euclid's response was destined to be paraphrased by teachers throughout the ages: "I am sorry, but there is no royal road to learning."

IT'S EASY TO SEE learning as an end result rather than an ongoing process. Once I get my diploma, certification, or job, it's all too natural to relax and feel that I should now enjoy the fruits of my labors. Therein lies the deadly trap of viewing learning (or change) as a phase, not a way of life.

Constant growth, development, and adaptability to change comes from lifelong learning. As the 19th-century British theologian and essayist John Henry Newman once said, "Growth is the only evidence of life." If we're not growing, we're like a dying tree; eventually the winds of change will snap us off our rotting trunks and blow us over.

LIKE CONTRIBUTING A FEW dollars a day to an investment fund, the habit of learning accumulates little by little, each day. How much we invest in that fund and where we invest it will determine how wealthy we eventually become.

Scottish author Samuel Smiles founded the modern self-help field with his 19th-century bestseller, *Self Help*. In it he writes: "Men of business are accustomed to quote the maxim that 'time is money' — but it is more; the proper improvement of it is self-culture, self-improvement, and growth of character. An hour wasted daily on trifles or in indolence, would, if devoted to self-improvement, make an ignorant man wise in a few years, and employed in good works, would make his life fruitful, and death a harvest of worthy deeds. Fifteen minutes a day devoted to self-improvement will be felt at the end of the year."

In the learning process, accidents and mistakes are often our best teachers.

Successful Failures

"To double your success rate, double your failure rate."

Tom Watson Sr., founder of IBM

In a small pub in the highlands of Scotland, a group of fishermen gathered one afternoon to swap tales over a round of ale. One of them stretched his arms apart to show the big one that got away. At that very point, a waitress walked past carrying a tray of full ale glasses. The fisherman's wild gestures sent the tray smashing against the wall. The dark brew splashed on the white wall of the pub and began running down. The waitress and the fisherman tried to wipe the mess off the wall, but it had left an ugly dark stain. A man who had watched the whole scene from another table walked quietly over to the wall. With a brown pastel crayon he took from his pocket, he began to sketch. The entire pub watched in silent awe as a majestic stag with great spreading antlers magically took shape around the stain. The artist was Sir Edwin Henry Landseer, the top 19th-century British painter of animals.

MANY DISCOVERIES AND BREAKTHROUGHS are made by accident. In fact, the history of innovation is a long list of failures that eventually led to bigger successes. There you'll find names like Post-It-Notes, Pyrex cookware, Jello, Popsicles, the Walkman, Lifesavers, Coca Cola, Silly Putty, Kleenex, Levi jeans, Band-Aids, Corn Flakes — and thousands more. Accidental innovations and unplanned applications happen every day. Few of them ever amount to anything productive and useful. But when inventors and companies are able to capitalize on their "happy accidents," it is because they are the most flexible and responsive to the unexpected opportunities before them. As 19th-century self-help pioneer Samuel Smiles wrote, "We often discover what will do, by finding out what will not do; and probably he who never made a mistake never made a discovery."

WHEN IT COMES TO sky diving, if at first I don't succeed…. my worries are over.

Few learning experiences are that deadly. However, learning-impaired people treat many new experiences as if they were. Fear of failure is a huge killer of innovation and learning. In *Measure for Measure*, William Shakespeare penned, "Our doubts are traitors/ And make us lose the good we oft might win/ By fearing to attempt."

If I am going to continue growing and developing, I have got to embrace the idea of trying something and failing. That will take me much further than doing nothing and succeeding. Life doesn't come with any guarantees. Nothing is certain. There is no such thing as a sure thing.

By taking few chances and not trying something new, I will reduce my risk of failure. I will also reduce my chances of success. As British author Katherine Mansfield implores us: "Risk! Risk anything! Care no more for the opinion of others, for those voices. Do the hardest thing on earth for you. Act for yourself."

One of my consulting firm's four core values is "High Growth and Development." (You can visit our web site at www.clemmer.net to read the others.) Here's how we express our expectations of each other and the people we consider adding to our team:

We are insatiable learners on a steep continuous personal growth curve. We have a good balance of active and reflective learning. Active learning comes from exploring, searching, creating, and experimenting. Reflective learning comes from taking time out of daily operational pressures to review how well our personal, team, and organizational improvement activities are working and to plan further changes. We are avid readers, researchers, and students in the fields of organization improvement, leadership development, and personal effectiveness.

We are highly innovative and very agile. We set short-term plans, but use strategic opportunism as we learn our way to new products and services. Our journey of discovery means we always have an abundance of trials, pilots, and experiments underway in our restless search for the pathways that will take us ever closer to our vision and purpose. We share what's working, and what's not, very openly with each other to advance our team and corporate knowledge and experience.

> *According to the theory of aerodynamics, as may be readily demonstrated through wind tunnel experiments, the bumblebee is unable to fly. This is because the size, weight, and shape of his body in relation to the total wingspread make flying impossible. But the bumblebee, being ignorant of those scientific truths, goes ahead and flies anyway — and makes a little honey every day.*

From an old poster found in a manufacturing plant

I CAME ACROSS THIS nugget of wisdom years ago. It's a favorite of mine, because it captures another key characteristic of learning leaders: they refuse to be trapped by "conventional wisdom" or what others say is or isn't possible.

Highly effective leaders go against the odds — or just ignore them. It's a trait that the legendary inventor Charles Kettering called "intelligent ignorance." Among his many teachings about innovation, he provides this useful perspective on growing and developing: "Research ... is nothing but a state of mind — a friendly, welcoming attitude toward change; going out to look for change instead of waiting for it to come. Research, for practical people, is an effort to do things better ... the research state of mind can apply to anything — personal affairs or any kind of business, big or little."

GROWING AND DEVELOPING

Leaders see beyond their own limitations — and those of others. They develop people into what they could be.

Lead to Succeed

> *A true Master is not the one with the most students, but one who creates the most Masters. A true leader is not the one with the most followers, but one who creates the most leaders.*

Neale Donald Walsch, *Conversations With God: An Uncommon Dialogue*

I was doing fairly well in Grades 1 to 3, especially in reading. Then, in Grade 4, I had a terrible teacher who made school so unhappy and unappealing that she almost caused me to drop out. (Of course, I would have waited another few years to make it official.) But in Grades 5 and 6, I was reclaimed by the nurturing of Mrs. Westman. I vividly remember her saying after I'd read a composition to the class, "Someday I won't be surprised to see your name on a book."

Her encouraging words simmered in my subconscious for years and helped me to see new possibilities for myself. Twenty years later my first book, *The VIP Strategy: Leadership Skills for Exceptional Performance*, was published. It was a real pleasure to present her with one of the very first copies — inscribed with a warm thank-you message. Her family and the local paper ensured that she got the recognition she so richly deserved.

MOST PEOPLE SEE OTHERS as they are; a leader sees them as they could be. Leaders like Mrs. Westman see beyond the current problems and limitations to help others see their own possibilities. It's a key part of their own growth and development.

We continue to grow when we help others grow and develop. That's the second half of the two-part cycle of growing and developing. (The first is our own growth and development, since we can't develop others if our own growth is stunted.) These two parts depend upon and support each other. We develop ourselves while we're developing others. By developing others, we develop ourselves further. This allows us to develop others still further.... the growth cycle spirals ever upward. The reverse is also true. By failing to develop myself and others, my growth and development cycle spins downward.

GROWING OTHERS

THE ART OF DEVELOPING others is the art of assisting their self-discovery. Writing in the 15th century, Galileo put it this way: "You cannot teach a man anything; you can only help him to find it within himself." As the ancient Chinese philosopher Lao-Tzu wrote: "Superior leaders get things done with very little motion. They impart instruction not through many words, but through a few deeds. They keep informed about everything but interfere hardly at all. They are catalysts, and though things would not get done as well if they weren't there, when they succeed they take no credit. And because they take no credit, credit never leaves them."

In the workplace, managers are generally considered to be responsible for helping employees to grow and develop. The traditional management view is to get work done through people, but strong leaders develop people through work.

As managers, team leaders, or team members, we can't be much help in developing others if we don't really know where they're trying to go. Once we understand that, we can work to align their development goals with those of the team or organization. They don't always match, but generally it's not too difficult to bring them together.

A similar approach applies to our parental leadership role with teenagers. The deepest love we can show our sons and daughters is to help them discover their unique purpose and uncover their special talents. That can be especially tough if it doesn't match the dreams we may have for them. Nevertheless, our leadership task is to help them be all that they can be, not what we would like to be if we were in their place.

Most often, leaders are ordinary people
with average talent. They just take that
talent to extraordinary levels.

Born to Lead?

Contrary to the myth that only a lucky few can ever decipher the
mystery of leadership, our research has shown us that leadership is
an observable, learnable set of practices....it's a process ordinary people
use when they're bringing forth the best from themselves and others.
Liberate the leader in everyone, and extraordinary things happen...
good leadership is an understandable and universal process.

James M. Kouzes and Barry Z. Posner,
The Leadership Challenge: How to Keep Getting
Extraordinary Things Done in Organizations

IN ANY FIELD OF endeavor, the final level of mastery is to make it look natural. That's a key reason why so many people believe achievement comes from winning the gene pool — either you're born with it or you're not. And certainly, a tiny number of athletes, performers, artists, musicians, or leaders do seem to succeed without really trying. But there's a much greater number of people — you probably know a few — who have tremendous natural talent and do very little with it.

More often than not, leaders are ordinary people with average talent who take it to extraordinary levels. Basketball superstar Michael Jordan, for example, wasn't even able to make his high school team. But through drive and determination, he was eventually able to develop his skills to legendary levels of performance.

As Mark Twain once said, "It usually takes me about three weeks to prepare a good impromptu speech." We don't see the thousands of hours of practice and study that world-class performers put into their work. When we do see the final performance, it looks so natural. "They're so lucky," we sigh.

It would be far more accurate for me to say, "I haven't chosen to become a great performer, athlete, writer, musician…...." That's perfectly legitimate. The intensity and focus ordinary people need to become extraordinary is well beyond the price most of us are willing to pay. It's much easier to surrender to the Victimitis Virus by saying to ourselves, "I am no good at speaking. Or writing. Or confronting issues. Or technology. Or being on time…."

British historian Edward Gibbon once noted a peculiar characteristic of what many people dismiss as luck: "The winds and the waves are always on the side of the best navigators." Our development is our choice. And our accumulated choices will either prepare us to take advantage of unexpected opportunities or they will weaken our abilities and set us up to be victims of change. Our leadership development choices raise us up or drag us down.

Learned Leadership

THE NATURE-VERSUS-NURTURE debate continues to rage in the field of leadership development. It's easy to be confused by those fascinating and rare individuals who are natural-born leaders. It doesn't help when books and articles on some of the more famous leaders gloss over their warts, personality quirks, doubts, and problems in reaching their high levels of achievement.

WARREN BENNIS HAS STUDIED hundreds of leaders in every field of human achievement, written over 20 books, and is professor and founding chair of the Leadership Institute at the University of Southern California. Bennis has concluded: "Biographies of great leaders sometimes read as if they entered the world with an extraordinary genetic endowment, as if their future leadership role was preordained. Do not believe it. The truth is that major capacities and competencies of leadership can be learned if the basic desire to learn them exists."

The ancient Greek orator Demosthenes provides an inspiring example of how we can choose to be leaders. Faced with the threat of a Macedonian conquest, he rallied his fellow citizens through his extraordinary abilities as a speaker — despite having a major speech impediment. He overcame this natural limitation by learning how to talk with pebbles in his mouth. He trained his voice by reciting speeches and verses while running or climbing steep hills. To force himself to stay inside to study and practise, he shaved half his head. (Today, of course, this might have made him a leader in the world of fashion!)

Another great orator, the Roman statesman and philosopher Cicero, came along about 100 years after Demosthenes. He provides leadership development advice that applies as much today as it did in 50 B.C. He listed "neglecting development and refinement of the mind, and not acquiring the habit of reading and study" as one of the six worst mistakes of humanity.

Being busy is not the same as being effective.
No matter how hectic life gets,
time spent thinking about the progress
of our growth is well worthwhile.

Reflection and Renewal

*Nay, be a Columbus to whole new continents and worlds
within you, opening new channels, not of trade, but of thought.*

Henry David Thoreau, *Walden*

In the 18th century, two explorers set forth with their ships to find the fabled Northwest Passage that cuts through the Arctic Circle across the top of North America, connecting the Atlantic and Pacific Oceans. Both men knew that the first to discover this elusive passage to China and India would find fame and fortune.

Captain John Smith was bold and impatient. He believed that speed was critical to winning the race against his rival, Captain Henry Jones. Captain Smith and his crew made record time through the ice-filled waters. They rarely consulted their charts and maps. They took only quick sextant readings to plot their position. They had no time or patience for such niceties, since they were too busy sailing their ships.

Meanwhile, Captain Jones and his crew kept a brisk pace, but took regular time out to check their progress against what little information was available in those vast, uncharted waters. They also studied the sea currents and charted wind directions. The captain and his officers met frequently to pool their information, debate what it all meant, and decide what direction they should take.

Had Captain Smith witnessed Jones's systematic approach, he would have laughed heartily. He was hundreds of miles ahead and making great time. But there was one small problem: he was heading into a deadly trap. He had ventured far down a sea lane that looked like an open passage — a passage that Captain Jones could have told him was a dead end, where the sea was about to

freeze over, and which was the most desolate, God-forsaken place in the Arctic.

But Jones was unaware of his rival's impending doom. He and his crew sailed steadily onward. As the seas froze, they wintered over in a well-protected area that had a good food supply. The next year they found the Pacific Ocean — and their fame and fortune.

The speedy Captain Smith and his crew were never heard from again. Decades later their frozen bodies and smashed ships were discovered by other explorers mapping the region.

THIS FICTIONAL STORY ILLUSTRATES a major problem we encounter again and again in our work with individuals, teams, and organizations trying to move to higher levels of performance. It's the problem of balancing the speed and pace of daily life or operations with periodically stepping back to make sure we're heading in the right direction.

Going nowhere in a hurry is a timeless leadership problem that's been with us for centuries. As the pace of change quickens, it's easier to fall into this age-old trap of confusing "busyness" with effectiveness. Like the wood-cutter who's too busy chopping to stop and sharpen his ax, we get caught up in a frantic pace that may be taking us to the wrong destination.

As Anglo-Irish playwright Oscar Wilde wrote in 1891, "We live in the age of the overworked, and the under-educated; the age in which people are so industrious that they become absolutely stupid." Over 100 years later, the tradition of industrious stupidity continues. If we're not paying close attention, we can get caught running flat out with our head down. We can race down dead-end roads and right over a cliff. We were too busy running to watch the signs or stop and look at a map.

STEPPING BACK, TAKING TIME out, assessing our direction and effectiveness, and reflecting on our progress is as rare as a proud man asking for directions. Here are a variety of perspectives showing how important reflection is to growing and developing:

The most excellent and divine counsel, the best and most profitable advertisement of all others, but the least practiced, is to study and learn how to know ourselves. This is the foundation of wisdom and the highway to whatever is good.
Pierre Charron, 16th-century French philosopher; *Of Wisdom*

We forge gradually our greatest instrument for understanding the world — introspection. We discover that humanity may resemble us very considerably — that the best way of knowing the inwardness of our neighbors is to know ourselves.
Walter Lippmann, Pulitzer Prize-winning American journalist and author

Self-reflection is the school of wisdom.
Baltasar Gracián, 17th-century Spanish author

With self-knowledge we lay the groundwork for the inner life without which we're slave to chance and circumstance.
Vincent Barry, *The Dog Ate My Homework: Personal Responsibility — How We Avoid it and What to do About it*

Self-reflection is the first key to becoming a leader.... leaders must be self-directed and self-reflective, listening to their inner voice and taking direction from their values and vision.
Warren Bennis and Joan Goldsmith, *Learning to Lead: A Workbook on Becoming a Leader*

GROWING POINTS

- The popular goals of security, stability, and predictability are deadly. The closer we get to these dangerous goals, the more our growth is stunted and learning reduced.

- True and lasting security comes from constant growth and development. We can't manage change, but we can be change *opportunists*.

- Our development is our choice. Those accumulated choices prepare us to take advantage of unexpected opportunities or weaken our abilities and set us up to be victims of change. Our leadership development choices raise us up or drag us down.

- What I am going to be tomorrow I am becoming today. To get somewhere else, I need to grow into someone else.

- Many discoveries and breakthroughs are made by accident. The inventors and companies that are able to capitalize on their "happy accidents" are those that are the most flexible and responsive to the unexpected opportunities before them.

- We continue to grow when we help others grow and develop. Most people see others as they are; a leader sees them as they could be. The art of developing others is the art of assisting their self-discovery.

- As the pace of change quickens, it's easy to fall into the age-old trap of confusing "busyness" with effectiveness. We can get caught up in a frantic pace that may be taking us to the wrong destination.

CHAPTER 8

PUTTING EMOTIONS IN MOTION

Leaders don't motivate with rewards and
punishments. Whether at home or
in the workplace, they energize people
to motivate themselves.

Mobilizing and Energizing

> *You never know when someone*
> *May catch a dream from you.*
> *You never know when a little word*
> *Or something you may do*
> *May open up the windows*
> *Of a mind that seeks the light...*
> *The way you live may not matter at all,*
> *But you never know, it might.*

Helen was running out of ideas. She had tried just about everything to get her two kids to help around the house. Her eldest, Tanya, was fourteen going on twenty-one. At age eleven, Justin seemed to be a noise covered in dirt. When they were younger, Helen could get them to do their jobs by enforcing strict rules or using threats and punishments. As the kids grew immune to that approach, Helen put down the stick and started to dangle rewarding carrots in front of them.

At one point, she developed a "star system." This involved putting a gold star beside the list on the fridge of each household chore they successfully completed. When they'd accumulated enough stars, they were rewarded with treats, cash bonuses, or special excursions. But the effectiveness of the rewards wore off and Helen had to become increasingly creative with new incentive programs. Ultimately, it had proved to be a losing battle: Tanya and Justin continued to lose interest in keeping the house neat and their chores completed. Helen found herself consistently nagging and yelling at them to get things done. They just didn't seem to care.

Paralleling Helen's frustration at home was what appeared to be a similar situation at the office: there, too, she had begun to notice that her group required an increasing variety of recognition programs and financial incentives to keep them motivated. Whenever a new compensation plan or recognition program was introduced, the team's energy level perked up and performance improved. But soon interest would wane, energy would drop, and performance would slip again. It seemed that everyone was more and more interested in "what's in it for me." Pride of accomplishment, satisfied customers, teamwork, and a sense of making a real difference faded into the background.

"Are rewards and punishments two sides of the same coin?" she wondered. "If so, it seems to be a coin that decreases in value the more it's used."

HELEN'S QUESTIONS AND OBSERVATIONS are on the right track. Far too many people try mobilizing and energizing by using different combinations of fear or greed. It's the lazy way out. These are superficial approaches that usually create major long-term problems.

In my firm's consulting and leadership development work, we are often asked for "how-to" approaches to improving morale or motivation. But low motivation or morale are symptoms of much deeper problems. The problem is rooted in combinations of Victimitis, inauthentic leadership, low levels of passion and commitment, lack of soul and meaning, weak energy levels, values misalignment, or fuzzy focus.

Certainly, people should be paid fairly. And profit- or gain-sharing programs are powerful ways to build partnerships and ownership. But leading with incentives (or punishments) to motivate others is often seen as manipulative. It reduces the value of doing the task for its own reward. It robs work of its meaning.

The key to effective motivation is building high-energy environments or experiences that inspire and mobilize people to action. That's tough work. There are no "cookie cutter" programs that can be dropped in to do it.

JACK WELCH HAS BEEN WIDELY called one of the most effective corporate leaders of his time. As CEO of General Electric, he transformed it into one of the world's largest, most profitable, and dynamic companies. World-renowned for leadership development, Welch declares simply, "If you can't energize others, you can't be a leader." He makes a vital point. All too often, the way many so-called leaders energize others is by leaving the room. Highly effective leaders energize others. That energy mobilizes people to action.

WE ARE EITHER PART of the energy problem or part of its solution. There is no neutral zone. We are either net takers or net contributors of energy to others. We need to ask those we're trying to lead or influence about our energy leadership. It is much less effective to force changes on others and overcome their resistance than to work collaboratively to build change partnerships.

There are many factors that mobilize and energize others. Some of the most important include appreciation, recognition, thanks, and celebration. These engender feelings of success that are addictive. We all want to feel like winners. We all want to feel we're making progress that's being noticed.

Our verbal communication skills also play a vital part in how effectively we can mobilize and energize others. Another key factor is participation and teamwork. Working together toward shared goals is very energizing.

Energizing people over the long term means going beyond appeals to fear and greed.

The Motivation Myth

It is the ultimate management conceit that we can motivate people.

Peter Scholtes, team effectiveness consultant and author

After six years at Universal Pictures, Harry Cohn formed Columbia Pictures in 1924. During the following decades he ran the company with an iron fist. His image as a tyrant was reinforced by the riding whip he kept near his desk to crack for emphasis. Cohn's form of "motivation" resulted in the greatest creative turnover of any major studio. At his funeral in 1958, one observer suggested that the 1,300 attendees "had not come to bid farewell, but to make sure he was actually dead."

Some parents want their kids to be independent as long as they do what they're told. Some managers want their people to be empowered as long as they follow directions.

We all know so-called leaders who believe that "motivation" is getting others to carry out their orders. They live by the philosophy that firings will continue until morale improves. Just do what you're told….and look like you're enjoying it. These forms of "motivation" are based on fear and force. If the punishment is strong enough and the policing rigid enough, they will lead to compliance.

PEOPLE WILL FOLLOW THE rules and marching orders. But that's all. Energy, creativity, and extra effort will be minimal. So will ownership and commitment. The only passion tyrants and autocrats create are fear, loathing, and the desire for revenge.

I ONCE SAW A Farcus cartoon that, for me, summed up the problem of the Motivation Myth. A manager is pictured at the head of a conference table addressing her department. The caption reads: "We need to improve morale. Any of you boneheads have a good idea?"

The main cause of the manager's problem seems pretty obvious. She just needs to look in the mirror. But the obvious isn't always so obvious. Root causes and symptoms are continuously confused. The manager is treating low morale as a problem to be solved rather than an indicator of much deeper issues. Clearly, those deeper problems include her contempt for her people, as well as her forceful personal style. Her approach is like an auto mechanic reporting, "I couldn't repair your brakes, so I made your horn louder."

WITH PROBLEMS OF MOTIVATION and morale, the distinction between symptoms and root causes can often be clarified by understanding the "doing versus being" aspects of mobilizing and energizing. We need to get beyond programs and techniques that take a "do to" approach. The big sticks of fear, punishments, and discipline — or the carrots of incentives and rewards — may work in the short term. But to sustain their effectiveness, we need to keep increasing the beatings or sweeten and vary the incentives. Eventually the beatings will burn people out and they will quit. Some will leave and find other jobs. Many will silently resign and continue to report for work every day.

People should be fairly rewarded for their contributions. The absence of money can be demotivating, but its presence doesn't provide healthy, long-term motivation. Using money or similar types of incentives to get increased performance turns people into self-centered mercenaries who are increasingly tuned into WIFM (what's-in-it-for-me). Pride, teamwork, concern for customers, shared values, growing and developing, passion, meaningful work, and the like fade. These become hollow words that raise "the snicker factor" whenever they are heard.

Effective mobilizing and energizing goes beyond "doing" programs to the "being" or culture of a family, community group, or organization. That culture is a set of shared attitudes and accumulated habits built around "the way we do things here." The culture provides the context or backdrop. And it's the culture that either energizes or exhausts people.

How energized are the people you seek to mobilize?

Energy Sources

"Your first and foremost job as a leader is to take charge of your own energy and then to help orchestrate the energy of those around you."

Peter Drucker, professor and author of dozens of books on economics, management, and leadership

IMAGINE RUSHING TO AN emergency room with severe stomach cramps. Without any examination, knowledge of your medical history, or questions about your symptoms, the doctor who has never seen you before says, "I know exactly what's wrong," and prescribes a powerful medication.

In the field of medicine, such treatment without diagnosis would be considered malpractice. The same is true in looking for ways to mobilize and energize others. There are many interconnected factors that inhibit or enhance energy. We can't really motivate others, but we can create high-energy environments that dramatically magnify and expand the energy of individuals, teams, or organizations.

In many ways, the Mobilizing and Energizing section of our leadership model (see page 18) is the product of all the other sections. The level of energy found in the people we're trying to mobilize depends largely on how effective we've been in the other dimensions of leadership. Let's examine each of these in turn.

Focus and Context

Our vision, values, and purpose are at the center of our being. They are also the wellspring from which our energy flows. Individuals, teams, and organizations with a strong sense of self, clear direction, and meaningful purpose have a high degree of energy. A fuzzy focus or cloudy context leads to a scattered life and diffused energy.

Responsibility for Choices

People who feel victimized and powerless don't have a lot of energy for change and improvement. Many teams, and sometimes whole organizations, can become badly infected with the Victimitis Virus. This often involves "blame storming" and developing excuses for not taking action since "it's not our fault." Turning this situation around often starts with getting people to see the problem and its paralyzing effects. Next steps may involve clarifying what is outside of our control, within our control, and what we can influence.

Authenticity

An environment that doesn't ring true with honesty, integrity, and trust is an environment that drains energy. The authenticity of my "changing me to change them" is a key element in maintaining that environment. It is supported by openness and constant feedback.

A young boy came home and told his Dad that the other kids kept stealing his pencils at school. The father stomped off to the school to complain. "It's the principle of the thing that bothers me most," he bellowed to his son's teacher. "It's not a matter of the pencils — I get plenty of those from work."

Benjamin Disraeli once wrote that "It was not reason that besieged Troy; it was not reason that sent forth the Saracen from the desert to conquer the world, that inspired the crusades, that instituted the monastic orders; it was not reason that produced the Jesuits; above all, it was not reason that created the French Revolution. Man is only great when he acts from the passions; never irresistible but when he appeals to the imagination."

Passion and Commitment

High-energy environments brim with passion and deep commitment. Humor and fun is often a key part of this. The laughter index is high and few people suffer from "jest lag."

Spirit and Meaning

Meaningless work that doesn't connect with a deeper part of us will drain energy. In recounting how his technology company, Lockheed Martin, survived and eventually prospered after an industry downturn reduced their revenues by 50%, CEO Norman Augustine points to a key principle in mobilizing and energizing others: "…the high sentiments always win in the end, the leaders who offer blood, toil, tears and sweat always get more out of their followers than those who offer safety and a good time. When it comes to the pinch, human beings are heroic."

Growing and Developing

When we align an individual's personal goals with those of the family, workgroup, or organization, we tap into huge energy reserves. It's similar to the healing process identified by the famous medical missionary, Dr. Albert Schweitzer: "The witch doctor succeeds for the same reason all the rest of us succeed. Each patient carries his own doctor inside him. They come to us not knowing the truth. We are best when we give the doctor who resides within each patient a chance to go to work." This alignment and energy expansion also comes from helping others constantly grow and develop.

Measuring your energy levels

At The CLEMMER Group, we designed the following Energy Index (EI) to help leaders dig deeper and uncover the root causes of why people they are trying to lead may not be mobilized and feel energized. The EI also points to areas that can be strengthened in order to further mobilize or energize a team or organization. The assessment is based on a five-point scale, where 1 is extremely weak and 5 is extremely strong.

Self-rating is a good place to start with the index. But the clearest picture will emerge by asking the group you're leading to rate each of these areas. Taking that courageous approach is the mark of a leader. It's a key part of building commitment and ownership.

❏   We see change as a new challenge and opportunity to grow

❏   We feel hopeful and optimistic and don't have the Victimitis Virus

❏   We take responsibility for our choices

❏   Our leaders are authentic and provide good examples to follow

❏   We operate with a high degree of honesty and integrity

❏   We give each other regular feedback on personal actions and behavior

❏   We have deep passion and commitment to our cause

❏   We take pride in, and joy from, our work

❏   We persist in the face of setbacks and failures

❏   We are self-disciplined

❏   Our work is meaningful and makes a difference

❏   We regularly devote time to learning and improvement

❏   Our leaders are highly effective coaches who help us develop

❏   We don't use threats, intimidation, or punishments

❏   Rewards are used to recognize and share success rather than as incentives to manipulate performance

❏   Our leaders have strong verbal communication skills

❏   Our group has many cooperative partnerships and strong relationships

❏   We frequently recognize, appreciate, and celebrate our small wins and significant successes

❏   We move beyond our "reality rut" of current problems to focus on what could be

❏   We have a strong and clear picture of our preferred future (vision)

❏   We have 3 or 4 principles (core values) that guide our behavior

❏   We have a strong sense of purpose

Scoring. 85+: the group is probably very energized. 60 to 84: not very strong; the lowest scoring areas need to be addressed if the team or organization is going to increase its energy and mobilization. 59 or less: there's probably a serious morale or motivation problem in the group or organization, and it's a deep-rooted problem that won't be quickly or easily fixed; increasing energy levels starts with systematically addressing the lowest-scoring areas.

Energy is fuelled less by the brain than the heart.

Emotional Intelligence

It is with the heart that one sees rightly; what is essential is invisible to the eye.

Antoine de Saint Exupéry, *The Little Prince*

OUR SOCIETY ADMIRES STRENGTH and power. Since the early games of the ancient Olympics, we've had contests of strength, stamina, speed, and the like. We've approached brain power or intellectual abilities in the same way.

We're in awe of intellectual giants with memory, reasoning, or complex problem-solving abilities far beyond our own. IQ tests were developed to measure this intellectual strength and power. We've come to believe that highly intelligent people make the best professors, doctors, managers, scientists, and so on. Many people believe that high IQ and high levels of success and happiness go together.

But many intellectual giants are emotional dwarfs. We all know people who can run mental circles around us lesser mortals, but their lives are a mess. Many do not suffer fools gladly. Their cutting wit or biting sarcasm often shows an arrogant, superior attitude that arouses resentment and reduces cooperation. This usually results in badly damaged relationships, organizations, or families.

SOMETHING IS MISSING. We know there's much more to a successful life than a strong head, we also need a strong heart. Intelligence is only part of the equation, we also need to deal with the human factors — the humanness in ourselves and others. We need to deal with emotional factors.

An exciting new field of study is emerging around what's being called "emotional intelligence." Many books, studies, and EQ-testing instruments are exploding on the scene. Daniel Goleman, psychologist, author, and *New York Times* journalist, got things going with his international bestseller, *Emotional Intelligence: Why It Can Matter More Than IQ*.

Here are some of the factors that Goleman sees as contributing to emotional intelligence: "...abilities such as being able to motivate oneself and persist in the face of frustrations; to control impulse and delay gratification; to regulate one's moods and keep distress from swamping the ability to think; to empathize and to hope."

That's a great definition of personal effectiveness. It's also a pretty good outline of many of the key leadership elements that we've been discussing throughout this book. At a leadership development workshop, I once introduced Goleman's definition. One of the participants was a sports psychologist who helps Olympic athletes improve their mental conditioning. He instantly responded to the quotation with the observation that it was a great definition of a world-class athlete.

As baseball legend Yogi Berra said, "Success in any sport is 90% physical skills and the other half is mental." (Nobody ever accused Yogi of being an intellectual giant — nor much of a mathematician — but he knew something about bringing our hands and head together with our heart.)

A well-researched book, *Emotional Intelligence* brings together the scientific proof that it's our attitude more than our aptitude that determines our altitude. Goleman's research leads him to conclude, "At best, IQ contributes about 20 percent to the factors that determine life success, which leaves 80 percent to other forces." This is overly conservative according to EQ researchers and authors Robert Cooper and Ayman Sawaf. In their book, *Executive EQ: Emotional Intelligence in Leadership & Organizations*, they write, ".... IQ may be related to as little as 4 percent of real-world success....over 90 percent may be related to other forms of intelligence... it is emotional intelligence, not IQ or raw brain power alone, that underpins many of the best decisions, the most dynamic and profitable organizations, and the most satisfying and successful lives."

Leaders energize others with optimism, encouraging them to see things as they could be.

Rays of Hope

If you ask [people] what they want in a leader, they usually list three things: direction or vision, trustworthiness, and optimism. Like effective parents, lovers, teachers, and therapists, good leaders make people hopeful.

Warren Bennis, *An Invented Life: Reflections on Leadership and Change*

Someone once remarked to television pastor Robert Schuller, "I hope you live to see all your dreams fulfilled."

"I hope not," Schuller replied, "because if I live and all my dreams are fulfilled, I'm dead. It's unfulfilled dreams that keep you alive."

HOPE IS ONE OF the most powerful sources of energy ever known to humankind. Without hope, we slip from living to just existing. Hope charges our spirit and draws us forward to a better tomorrow. Hope helps us see beyond the problems to the possibilities. Hope gives life meaning. Hope helps us take responsibility for our choices. Hope stretches us and energizes our continuous growth and development. Hope urges us to go against the odds and do what everyone knows can't be done.

All the great achievements and tiny triumphs recorded through the history of civilization began as a hope — a dream in someone's mind. An ancient Chinese proverb teaches that "happiness is someone to love, something to do, and something to hope for."

The phrase "false hope" is really a contradiction in terms. Hope can't be false. It might be unfulfilled, but it can't be false. If hope makes me try a little longer, strive a little further, live a little more, dream a little more clearly, or raise my expectations a little higher, how can it be false?

But in the face of despair, negativity, and feelings of helplessness, being hopeful is hard work. It's easier to reflect a negative environment and be a pessimist. It doesn't take as much effort to give up hope and become a victim. Then it's somebody else's fault. It doesn't take much courage to be a cynic who sees things only as they are, not as they could be.

The 19th-century American abolitionist Henry Ward Beecher defined the feeble-mindedness of the pessimist or cynic as "one who never sees a good quality in a man and never fails to see a bad one. He is the human owl, vigilant in darkness and blind to light, mousing for vermin, and never seeing noble game. The cynic puts all human actions into two classes — openly bad and secretly bad."

A leader brings hope. That doesn't mean putting on rose-colored glasses, painting on a happy face, and avoiding problems by spouting clichés on positive thinking. Highly effective leaders help others deal with the reality of current problems by focusing their attention on what's possible. They use the dream of *what could be* as a magnet to draw everyone forward.

Highly energized cultures are charged with hopefulness and optimism. It's the dynamic power that mobilizes people to make the improbable possible. It's the mark of a leader.

Compelling communication is essential to energizing and mobilizing others.

Words Worth

> *The man who can think but does not know how to express what he thinks is at the same level as he who cannot think.*

Pericles, leader of Athens circa 450 B.C.

It was the dead of winter in the middle of a very cold snap. As we approached departure time, judging by all the activity outside the aircraft, we weren't likely to leave on time. In a few minutes the captain announced, "You can see a lot of activity on our left wing. This is a maintenance crew trying to replace a defective fuel pump. We find it's best to fix a problem like that on the ground before we're in the air. The good news is that there is another fuel pump available here at the airport. The bad news is that it will delay our departure by about 30 minutes."

Within 10 minutes the captain was making another announcement, "Folks, you can see the little truck on the right coming in with our fuel pump. Unfortunately, this is work that can only be done with gloves off. Working with jet fuel on your fingers in this freezing weather is extremely difficult and taking longer than expected." We started to feel sorry for those hearty heroes working in such tough conditions to get us underway!

The captain continued to give us updates on progress every 10 to 15 minutes. When he announced the problem was fixed and we were finally ready to go — some 90 minutes late — a cheer went up from the passengers.

As late as we were, I am sure there wasn't a single complaint among my fellow passengers. That's because the captain treated us like adult customers — not "the cattle in the back" who don't really need to know what's going on.

COMMUNICATION IS ONE OF the key marks of a leader. Like motivation, it's also a word that's overused and misunderstood. For example, what are often called "communication problems" in many groups or organizations are really problems of process, system, or structure. People don't communicate because the way they are organized doesn't let them do it effectively.

The strength of our communications spring, in part, from our personal values. The airline captain communicated with us from values that said we were important enough and responsible enough to be told what was going on — even if the news was bad.

If my values include a sense of superiority over others, I won't bother communicating with "the peons." If I am arrogant, I may call my loud, one-way horn-blowing "communication." If I have disdain for others, the only thing my tone of voice may arouse is resentment, hostility, or defensiveness.

If I see customers, suppliers, or organization members in other departments as interruptions or adversaries rather than people, I'll brush them off with minimum effort. If I am suspicious and distrustful, I will parcel out information on a "need to know" basis. If I think all the EQ (emotional intelligence) research is hogwash, I won't bother to develop my verbal communication skills.

With few exceptions, highly effective leaders have very strong verbal (and often written) communication skills. They connect with people. Since leadership deals with emotions, energy, and spirit, verbal communication skills have a huge role to play in mobilizing and energizing.

No matter how "right" a vision, deeply held principles, or purpose may be, they won't mobilize others if they can't be effectively communicated. That means moving beyond dry logic, sterile printed statements, or speeches read with all the passion of a bored old professor giving the same old lecture to a group of equally bored young students.

Highly effective leaders transfer their energy and passion to the people they're trying to mobilize with words that paint exciting pictures, ring true, fire the imagination, or touch the spirit. Like the leader, their words are charged with energy.

Celebration and appreciation is a powerful energy source.

Giving Thanks

We believe that what is rewarding gets done.
We can never pay people enough to care — to care
about their products, services, communities,
or families, or even the bottom line.
True leaders tap into people's hearts and
minds, not merely their hands and wallets.

James M. Kouzes and Barry Z. Posner,
The Leadership Challenge: How to Keep Getting
Extraordinary Things Done in Organizations

Arden Barker had planted a 50-acre field of wheat that was now golden-brown, very full, and ready for harvest. It was a sight to touch the heart of any farmer. When his Uncle Harry came to visit, Arden proudly took him out to look at the field of wheat. Harry looked around, put his hand over his eyes to peer into the distance, and fixed his gaze on a boulder that had been too large to move in the middle of the field. "Is that a stone on the hill?" he asked. He said nothing about the field of wheat. Arden was crushed by his lack of enthusiasm.

The Uncle Harry incident became the subject of discussion at many Barker family dinners thereafter. A few years later, their daughter, Brenda, had just finished cutting and trimming the family's huge lawn. Arden came home and surveyed her work from the kitchen window. "You missed a patch under the trees," he pointed out. Brenda came over to him, put one arm around his waist, and her other hand over her eyes to peer off into the distance and asked, "Is that a stone on the hill?"

Highly effective leaders energize others by noticing and recognizing the field of wheat — not the stone. They thank, appreciate, recognize, and celebrate accomplishments.

We all draw a lot of energy from sincere recognition and honest appreciation. It's like a warm ray of sunshine. On the other hand, we all know (and dread) the compulsive critics who carry big magnifying glasses around to get a good close look at everyone's imperfections. They seem to feel that their mission in life is to ignore the golden field of wheat and point out the stones on the hill. As bosses their attitude is "Your recognition is you get to keep your job." As spouses it's "Of course I love you; I married you, didn't I?" As parents it's "you're doing fine because you're not being punished or asked to leave."

One study showed that 46% of people who quit their jobs did so because they felt unappreciated. No doubt as many kids and spouses gave up on their families for the same reason. A key leadership question is whether we're building a "thank you" or "spank you" culture.

Paul thought he wasn't doing well because he never got any feedback and his boss seemed constantly dissatisfied with his work. So he began looking for another job. As he was getting close to leaving, the company had a big conference. Paul was given a gold pen and honored for his outstanding contributions. After "doing his recognition thing," the next day Paul's boss went right back to treating Paul like a piece of furniture. Paul redoubled his efforts to find another job. A few months later, he was gone to a company that showed their appreciation more than once every year or two.

IT'S ALL TOO EASY to confuse our positive feelings or good intentions about others with actually expressing our appreciation for their contributions. But unexpressed good feelings mean nothing to anyone else. In other cases, we wait for formal recognition activities rather than giving more frequent and personal positive feedback.

Our energy levels are charged from internal and external sources. Highly self-directed people have strong inner resources from which they draw their energy. But most people's energy levels are highly dependent on the responses they get from others, such as teachers, parents, spouses, bosses, team members, or peers that they look to for direction or support. Too many people drain the energy of others with criticism, pessimism, and apathy. Highly effective leaders boost the energy of others with their optimism, passion, and appreciation. They work hard to give people early and frequent tastes of success. The recognition and celebration recharges everyone and makes them eager to do more.

Little Cindy, a seven-year-old optimist, provides a good model of the balance between striving for ever-bigger roles in life while also appreciating the roles we get. Cindy was trying out for a part in a school play. Her mother said she really had set her heart on being in it, though she was afraid that Cindy would not be chosen.

On the day the parts were awarded, Cindy rushed up to her mother when she came to pick her up. Cindy's eyes were shining with pride and excitement. "Guess what, Mom?" she shouted, "I've been chosen to clap and cheer."

OUR OWN FEELINGS OF accomplishment are often matters of perception. It's easy to focus on what we haven't yet achieved. We can drain our own energy by dwelling on our setbacks and disappointments.

Being part of a strong group energizes each member of that group.

The Power of Participation

Teams help ordinary people achieve extraordinary results.

A certain man had several sons who were always quarreling with one another, and, try as he might, he could not get them to live together in harmony. So he determined to convince them of their folly by the following means. Bidding them fetch a bundle of sticks, he invited each in turn to break it across his knee. All tried and all failed. Then he undid the bundle, and handed them the sticks one by one, when they had no difficulty at all in breaking them. "There, my boys," he said, "united, you will be more than a match for your enemies; but if you quarrel and separate, your weakness will put you at the mercy of those who attack you." Union is strength.

As this Aesop fable illustrates, even weaker people are powerful when united in a strong team. It's one of the most effective ways to mobilize and energize people. Teams are a key way to get people participating and involved. That leads to higher levels of ownership, commitment — and energy.

Numerous studies of change and improvement efforts in North American organizations have shown that major gains in quality, service, or productivity are driven by huge increases in participation and involvement levels throughout those successful organizations.

Effective team leaders develop a group from what it is into the team that it could be. That takes a focus and skill set that is new and different for most team members and leaders.

Since the beginning of the industrial age, group leadership has been based on the military model of command and control. We managed groups by pushing and forcing them. At best, we got compliance and conformity. At worst, we set up huge "we/they" gaps that lead to union/management conflict and lots of other problems. Group ownership, shared goals, creativity, and participation were minimal. In the bad old days, the boss's idea of participation was like the kid who rode the sled downhill and "shared" it with others in his group by letting them take it back up again.

Today's highly effective teams have a broad ownership and participation in the team's tasks and how everyone works together to achieve them. Team members and leaders share responsibility for the effectiveness of the team. One of the best indicators of the strength of a team is the "We to Me" ratio. How often do team members and leaders use words like "we" and "ours" instead of "I" or "me" and "mine" in their conversations?

Despite all the "team talk" of recent years, the fact is that few groups today are real teams. Too often they're unfocused and uncoordinated in their efforts. It's a problem that my firm has encountered time and time again in our consulting work, which is why we developed the set of questions shown at left. This team assessment and planning framework is designed to help newly formed teams come together and get productive quickly — or to assist existing teams in refocusing and renewing themselves.

Teams develop answers and related action plans around each question. This approach has proven to be much more effective than artificial team situations, outdoor adventures, or theoretical discussions of group dynamics. Bringing a team together with a shared focus and taking action to make it happen is a powerful way to mobilize and energize.

❏ Why do we exist (our purpose)?

❏ Where are we going (our vision)?

❏ How will we work together (our values)?

❏ Whom do we serve (internal or external customers or partners)?

❏ What is expected of us?

❏ What are our performance gaps (difference between the expectations and our performance)?

❏ What are our goals and priorities?

❏ What's our improvement plan?

❏ What skills do we need to develop?

❏ What support is available?

❏ How will we track our performance?

❏ How/when will we review, assess, celebrate, and refocus?

GROWING POINTS

- There are many interconnected factors that inhibit or enhance energy. We can't really motivate others directly, but we can create high-energy environments that dramatically magnify and expand the energy of individuals, teams, or organizations.

- Effective mobilizing and energizing goes well beyond "doing" programs to the "being" or culture of a team, organization, or any group, including a family. That culture is a set of shared attitudes and accumulated habits around "the way we do things here." The culture provides the context or backdrop that either energizes or exhausts people.

- We use our intellect or IQ to manage with the head. We use our emotions or emotional intelligence (EQ) to lead with the heart. EQ is much more important than IQ in predicting personal or organizational success.

- Hope is one of the most powerful sources of energy ever known to humankind. Highly effective leaders help others deal with the reality of current problems by focusing their attention on what's possible.

- Highly effective leaders have very strong verbal (and often written) communication skills. They transfer their energy and passion to the people they're trying to mobilize with words that paint exciting pictures, ring true, fire the imagination, or touch the spirit.

- Highly effective leaders boost the energy of others with their optimism, passion, and appreciation. They thank, appreciate, recognize, celebrate, and work hard to give people early and frequent tastes of success. This recharges everyone and makes them eager to do more.

- Teams are a key way to get people participating and involved. That leads to higher levels of ownership, commitment — and energy. Team members and leaders share responsibility for the effectiveness of the team. One of the best indicators of the strength of a team is the "We to Me" ratio.

TAKING ACTION

When is the best time to embark on our leadership development journey? How about today?

Grow for It

> *Mr. Meant-To has a comrade,*
> *And his name is Didn't-Do;*
> *Have you ever chanced to meet them?*
> *Did they ever call on you?*
> *These two fellows live together*
> *In the house of Never-Win,*
> *And I'm told that it is haunted*
> *By the ghost of Might-Have-Been.*

William J. Bennett, *The Book of Virtues*

A recurring nightmare haunted Peter to re-examine and change the aimless and drifting course of his life. In his bad dream he was standing before a severe judge and disapproving jury. "You are charged with wasting your life," the judge bellowed harshly down to Peter standing before the high bench. "How do you plead?"

Restraining himself from fleeing the courtroom, Peter was finally forced to whisper, "Guilty." He appeared ready to say more, then stood lost in thought.

The clock ticked steadily on the courthouse wall. "I always had the best of intentions," Peter began slowly. "I just never got around to translating them into action. There was always tomorrow. But tomorrow never came and the world went speeding by. I ran out of time. I guess, after all is said and done, a lot has been said, but only a little has been done."

LOOKING BACK, WE CAN all point to times in our lives that seem wasted. In some cases, those times were a pause in the action. Perhaps it was time to regroup and take a different course or rest before trying again. The danger is if the time-out turns into just-putting-in-time.

If we fail to continuously grow, change, and develop, then precious life is wasted. As the American writer Elbert Hubbard warned, "The recipe for perpetual ignorance is to be satisfied with your opinions and content with your knowledge."

Imagine there is a bank that
Credits your account each morning with $86,400.
It carries over no balance from day to day.
Every evening it deletes whatever part of the balance
You failed to use during the day.
What would you do?
Draw out every cent, of course!
Each of us has such a bank.
Its name is TIME.

Every morning, it credits you with 86,400 seconds.
Every night it writes off as lost whatever of this you
Have failed to invest to good purpose.
It carries over no balance.
It allows no overdraft.
Each day it opens a new account for you.
Each night it burns the day's deposits; the loss is yours.

There is no going back.
There is no drawing against the "tomorrow."
You must live in the present on today's deposits.
Invest it so as to get from it the utmost in health,
Happiness, and success!
The clock is running.
Make the most of today.

Treasure every moment that you have!
And remember that time waits for no one.
Yesterday is history.
Tomorrow is a mystery.
Today is a gift.
That's why it's called, "the present."

Anonymous

Success isn't measured by how far we've got,
but by the distance we've traveled
from where we started.

Am I Growing the Distance?

*After climbing a great hill, one only finds that
there are many more hills to climb. I have taken a moment here
to rest, to steal a view of the glorious vista that surrounds me,
to look back on the distance I have come. But I can rest
only for a moment, for with freedom comes responsibilities,
and I dare not linger, for my long walk is not yet ended.*

Nelson Mandela, *Long Walk to Freedom*

TO KNOW IF I am growing the distance, I need to be able to answer three basic questions:

1. Where do I want to go?

2. Where am I now?

3. What do I need to change or improve to close the gap?

Let's recap how we find the answers.

Question 1.

Where do I want to go?

MANY PEOPLE KNOW WHAT they *don't* want; far fewer know what they *do* want.

Confucius said, "If one takes no thought about what is distant, he will find sorrow near at hand." Failing to stake out our preferred future and steadily work toward that distant dream is one reason "sudden changes" take so many people by surprise. The resulting crisis can be especially devastating when we're not focused on what we ultimately want to achieve.

It takes a lot of hard and constant work to understand where we want to go. It's wrapped up with what we believe in and why we exist. That's why vision, values, and purpose form the interconnected Focus and Context that is at the center of our being (and our leadership model; see page 18). I hope this book has brought you closer to answering these core questions and defining your distance at this stage of your life's journey.

If you'd like further "how to" steps and ideas on Focus and Context, see chapters 7 to 9 in my previous book, *Pathways to Performance*; you'll find dozens of pointers and suggestions ("Pathways and Pitfalls"). For more reference information, see the Appendix of this book on page 181.

Question 2.

Where am I now?

UNDERSTANDING WHERE I AM now is also a big challenge. It calls for the courage and honesty to squarely face my strengths and my weaknesses, my successes and my setbacks. It means I need to combine inner reflection with outer feedback. That's not easy. It's far easier to be a victim and blame others for where I am in my life right now.

Life is Change

"I hate all this change," Dirk shouted angrily at the TV news anchor. "Why can't things just stay the same?" He threw a pillow at the TV screen and clicked it off with a snort.

Suddenly a hissing noise arose from the corner of the room and green, shimmering mist filled the air. Dirk stood in shock as a one-foot-tall, wrinkled old man emerged from the glowing cloud. The tiny, grizzled fellow had a long flowing white beard and was dressed from head to toe in green. His eyes twinkled with mischief as he flashed a gap-toothed grin. "Hi, I am Mike. I can take you to a place where people don't have to deal with change and things stay the same all the time."

Before Dirk could say a word, the little elf drew a handful of sparkling green dust from his vest pocket. With an impish smirk and a big wink, he threw the powder at Dirk. With the hissing sound filling his hears, Dirk was engulfed in the green, twinkling fog. Still unable to see through the emerald haze, he heard Mike say, "Here we are. Here's a place where things stay the same and people don't have to deal with change."

The elf blew away the mist. They were standing on the lush green grass of a well-trimmed graveyard. Neat, polished gravestones stretched far out to the horizon.

Continued on next page...

As the Italian writer Ugo Betti put it, "This free will business is a bit terrifying. It's almost pleasanter to obey, and make the most of it."

It's also easier to delude myself into believing I am further along my path than I really am. I hope *Growing the Distance* has helped to enrich your personal assessment and increase your awareness of where you are now.

Question 3.

What do I need to change or improve to close the gap?

Weep not that the world changes. Did it keep a stable, changeless state, it were cause indeed to weep.

William Cullen Bryant, 19th-century American poet and critic

As I POINTED OUT in Chapter One ("The Way of the Leader"), we can't manage change. For historical proof, we need look no further than the collapse of the old Soviet Union — probably the single biggest "change management" failure of the 20th century. With highly centralized planning, the politburo tried to control the lives of an entire block of nations. There were to be few surprises and activities that weren't in the official plan. Bureaucratic organizations often try to do the same thing. So do many static, low-growth individuals. We need to be on guard against our own rigid thinking and "hardening of the attitudes."

The faster the world changes around us, the further behind we fall by just standing still. If the rate of external change exceeds our rate of internal growth, just as the day follows night, we will surely be changed. To the change-blind, with their stunted growth, it will happen suddenly and seemingly "out of the blue."

(Continued from page 173)

"Life is change," the aged elf said with a chuckle as he leapt to the top of a headstone. "It's one of nature's mighty laws. Eons ago I had this conversation with my old buddy, Heraclitus, and told him that change is the only thing that's permanent."

The elf grimaced playfully. "Of course, he took the credit for saying that."

"Anyway," he continued, "it's a timeless principle. People who aren't changing and growing aren't living. Growth is one of nature's vital signs. It shows you're alive. Once you stop changing and growing, you'd better check your pulse."

Change forces choices. If we're on the grow, we'll embrace many changes and find the positive in them. It's all in where we choose to put our focus. Even change that hits us in the side of the head as a major crisis can be full of growth opportunities — if we choose to look for them. I hope *Growing the Distance* helps you move further toward embracing and thriving on change. It's key to a rich and full life.

WE DON'T ALWAYS GET to choose the changes that come into our lives. But we do get to choose how to respond.

In my workshops and speaking engagements, when working with people who feel under siege by negative, unwanted change, I often show the Chinese symbol for "crisis." It provides a stark example of the timeless importance of making choices. Apparently, the top character in the two-part symbol reads as darkness, disaster, and danger. The bottom character reads as opportunity, renewal, and rebirth. (It could be a lot of swearing for all I know; but I have had this interpretation confirmed by a number of people who can read Chinese.)

Many people or organizations who have successfully weathered a serious crisis — at least, those who didn't give in to the dark forces of despair and Victimitis — look back years later and point to that event as a significant turning point. Most would rather not go through that pain again, but it was a key part of their growth.

Crisis can be a danger that weakens or destroys us. Or crisis can be a growth opportunity. The choice is ours. Whichever we choose — we're right about that crisis. We make it our reality.

Change is life. Successfully dealing with change means choosing to continuously grow and develop. Failing to grow is failing to live.

Each of us has to struggle along our own path to personal growth. The effort, although sometimes painful, makes us stronger.

Personal Pathways

The process of spiritual growth is an effortful and difficult one. This is because it is conducted against a natural resistance, against a natural inclination to keep things the way they were, to cling to the old maps and old ways of doing things, to take the easy path.

M. Scott Peck, *The Road Less Traveled*

THROUGHOUT *Growing the Distance*, I have emphasized that we all need to be leaders. Personal, career, and family success is a product of strong leadership. Leadership is an action, not a position. It's a way of being that moves from the inside out to guide our way of doing things.

A timeless principle of inside-out leadership is found in continuous personal growth. When U.S. Supreme Court associate justice Oliver Wendell Holmes Jr. was hospitalized at the age of 92, President Roosevelt went to visit him. He found Holmes reading a Greek primer. "Why are you reading that?" the president asked. The great jurist replied, "Why, Mr. President, to improve my mind."

CONTINUOUS PERSONAL IMPROVEMENT means we often outgrow our own standards and what we previously thought was acceptable. A dull author once complained to William Dean Howells, a 19th-century editor of the *Atlantic Monthly* (he encouraged a number of writers, including Mark Twain and Henry James), "I don't seem to write as well as I used to."

"Oh yes, you do...indeed you do," Howells reassured him, "It's your taste that is improving."

WE NEED TO FIND the right combination of activities — reflection, networking, participating in learning events, training, discussions, taking on new assignments and responsibilities, experimenting, or whatever — to keep us stretching and growing.

Reading is a powerful way to stretch our minds and keep growing. Not all readers are leaders, but most lifelong leaders are avid readers. A Gallup poll found that high-income people read an average of 19 books per year. That compares to 1.9 books per year in the general population — a 10-fold difference!

Charles William Eliot served as president of Harvard University during the 19th century. Of books, he said, "[they] are the quietest and most constant of friends; they are the most accessible and wisest of counselors, and the most patient of teachers."

"Reading is to the mind what exercise is to the body," declared the 18th-century writer, Sir Richard Steele. I heartily agree. As an author, of course, I'll admit to a little bias on the subject. I encourage you to look at my recommended reading list on page 182.

The Moth

A man found the cocoon of an emperor moth. He took it home so that he could watch the moth come out of the cocoon. On that day a small opening appeared; he sat and watched the moth for several hours as it struggled to force its body through that little hole.

Then it seemed to stop making any progress. It appeared as if it had gotten as far as it could and it could go no farther. It just seemed to be stuck.

Then the man, in his kindness, decided to help the moth, so he took a pair of scissors and snipped off the remaining bit of the cocoon. The moth then emerged easily. But it had a swollen body and small, shriveled wings.

The man continued to watch the moth because he expected that, at any moment, the wings would enlarge and expand to be able to support the body, which would contract in time.

Neither happened. In fact, the little moth spent the rest of its life crawling around with a swollen body and shriveled wings. It never was able to fly.

What the man in his kindness and haste did not understand was that the restricting cocoon and the struggle required for the moth to get through the tiny opening was the way of forcing fluid from the body of the moth into its wings so that it would be ready for flight once it achieved its freedom from the cocoon.

Freedom and flight would only come after the struggle.

By depriving the moth of a struggle, he deprived the moth of health. Sometimes struggles are exactly what we need in our life. If we were to go through our life without any obstacles, we would be crippled. We would not be as strong as we could have been.

Anonymous

CONTINUOUS LEARNING, GROWING, and developing helps us find the path that is personal and unique to each of us. Ways of doing things — whether that's operating a machine, using a software program, dealing with a customer, managing a process, cooking a meal, or resolving a conflict — depend upon tools and techniques. But there are no tools or techniques for ways of being. We all need to keep searching, growing, and developing those ways that are true to our inner selves and take us where we want to go.

There are no quick-and-easy formulas to leadership development. In his book, *The Heart Aroused*, poet David Whyte illustrates how difficult it can be to find our own way: "In my experience, the more true we are to our own creative gifts the less there is an outer reassurance or help at the beginning. The more we are on the path, the deeper the silence in the first stages of the process. Following our path is in effect a kind of going off the path, through open country, there is a certain early stage when we are left to camp out in the wilderness, alone, with few supporting voices. Out there in the silence we must build a hearth, gather the twigs, and strike the flint for the fire ourselves...if we can see the path laid out for us, there is a good chance it is not our path: it is probably someone else's we have substituted for our own. Our own path must be deciphered every step of the way."

Success requires thought *and* action.

Get Growing

A CALL TO ACTION

> *A parrot talks much but flies little.*

Wilbur Wright, American aviation pioneer

WHY DO SOME PEOPLE fail to grow the distance?

Some people fail because they *do* but don't *think*. They are like the hyperactive entrepreneur who burst into a travel agent's office and urgently demanded a ticket. "Where do you want to go?" the agent asked him. "I don't care," he retorted breathlessly. "Just give me a ticket! I've got business everywhere!" Since an action is only as strong as its "weakest think," I hope *Growing the Distance* is helping you think more deeply about where you want to go, where you are now, and what you need to grow next.

On the other hand, many unsuccessful people *think* but don't *do*. These people know all the theories. They can quote chapter, verse, phrase, and story from leadership and personal effectiveness books, magazines, and speakers. They are walking professors of personal growth. But their experiences are all conceptual. They know, but don't act on their knowledge. They are like an "expert" in love and marriage who has never even had a date.

What Seeds Are We Planting?

A farmer prayed fervently every night for a fine crop. He pleaded for crops as fine as his neighbor's. After one night of particularly vigorous prayer, the Lord finally replied: "Ben, how can I give you a harvest? You didn't plant any seeds last spring."

Now is the time to prepare for our next harvest. We can't wait until harvest time to plant the seeds. We can't strike a bargain to plant seeds once we see whether the harvest is worth the effort. Harvest time will arrive whether we're ready or not. Now is the time to plant the seeds for the coming harvests.

NOW IS THE TIME for action. Now is the time to move from where we are to where we want to be. Now is the time to grow toward our distant dreams. That takes courage and discipline. It's far easier to be a victim and fall back on excuses — we're too old, it's too late, we've missed our big chances in life, or today's opportunities aren't as good as they used to be.

Such Victimitis leads straight to Pity City. If we're not careful, we'll grow increasingly bitter and resistant to change as we regret what might have been. If we're going to live to the fullest, we need to be thoroughly used up before we leave this earth. Countless people through the ages who awoke late in life have shown that it's never too late.

There's still time. If not now, when?

Perseverance

We must not hope to be mowers,

And to gather the ripe gold ears,

Unless we have first been sowers

And watered the furrows with tears.

It is not just as we take it,

This mystical world of ours,

Life's field will yield as we make it

A harvest of thorns or of flowers.

Johann Wolfgang von Goethe

LET'S STAY IN TOUCH

AS THE FROG SAID while he sat on the lily pad, "Time's fun when you're having flies." As you've been reading *Growing the Distance*, the skies may not have parted to reveal the angelic hosts conveying some blinding new insight to you. Even so, if you found some or all of this book useful, please let me and other readers know what was meaningful and what you've done as a result. I'd really like to know what insights or experiences *Growing the Distance* triggered for you.

In the meantime, may you keep growing day by day. May you never close the gap between where you are and where you want to be.

May you keep growing the distance.

Take advantage of substantial discounts when you purchase multiple copies of *Growing the Distance*

A VALUABLE RESOURCE FOR EVERYONE IN YOUR ORGANIZATION

Although highly applicable to people with roles and titles like manager, supervisor, or executive, *Growing the Distance* also appeals to a much broader audience. The book was written to be distributed in quantity by executives, managers, and training professionals attempting to help people throughout their organizations:

- embrace personal growth and development as a key to dealing with continuous and unpredictable change
- provide a strong base for leadership development programs
- build a common foundation of values around its timeless principles
- establish a broader "context of being" for training programs teaching technical, process, or behavioral "skills of doing"
- bring teams together with a common language and set of values
- help everyone in the organization become leaders
- nurture ongoing personal growth and development

Growing the Distance also makes a great gift for:
- young people getting started in life
- someone contemplating career changes and choices
- people wrestling with major change or a crisis
- someone who's lost their job or had it dramatically changed
- people feeling unfocused and listless
- managers, entrepreneurs, and executives looking to increase their leadership effectiveness
- people "on the grow" always looking for personal development
- customers, suppliers, distributors, dealers, and other partners

Major discounts are available for multiple copies of *Growing the Distance*. Visit The CLEMMER Group's website (www.clemmer.net) or call toll-free 1-888-925-GROW (4769) for more information.

JIM'S RECOMMENDED READING LIST

The following books are leading edge, old favorites, or classics hand-picked from my personal library. I have found them especially helpful in my writing, consulting, business building, and personal development. In the Recommended Resources section of our web site (www.clemmer.net), you will find many more recommended books. I periodically update the list with new recommendations. I hope some of these books help you to continue growing your distance.

Personal Development

Barry, Vincent. *The Dog Ate My Homework: Personal Responsibility - How We Avoid It and What to Do About It.* Kansas City: Andrews and McMeel, 1997.

Bolles, Richard Nelson. *What Color is Your Parachute? A Practical Manual for Job Hunters and Career Changers.* (Annual Edition). Berkeley: Ten Speed, (Updated Annually).

Bolles, Richard N. *The Three Boxes of Life and How to Get Out of Them: An Introduction to Life/Work Planning.* Berkeley: Ten Speed, 1981.

Bristol, Claude M. *The Magic of Believing.* New York: Pocket, 1969.

Bristol, Claude M. and Harold Sherman. *TNT: The Power Within You.* Englewood Cliffs: Prentice-Hall, 1954.

Carnegie, Dale. *How to Stop Worrying and Start Living.* New York: Simon and Schuster, 1975.

Carnegie, Dale. *How to Win Friends and Influence People.* New York: Simon and Schuster, 1964.

Carnegie, Dale. *The Quick and Easy Way to Effective Speaking.* Rev. ed. Ed. Dorothy Carnegie. Garden City: Carnegie, 1977.

Carnegie, Dorothy. *Don't Grow Old - Grow Up!* New York: Dutton, 1956.

Covey, Stephen R. *The Seven Habits of Highly Effective People: Restoring the Character Ethic.* New York: Simon and Schuster, 1989.

Covey, Stephen R., A. Roger Merrill and Rebecca R. Merrill. *First Things First: To Live, to Love, to Learn, to Leave a Legacy.* New York: Simon and Schuster, 1994.

Csikszentmihalyi, Mihaly. *Flow: The Psychology of Optimal Experience.* New York: HarperPerennial, 1991.

Garfield, Charles. *Peak Performers: The New Heroes of American Business.* New York: Morrow, 1986.

Garfield, Charles A. with Hal Zina Bennett. *Peak Performance: Mental Training Techniques of the World's Greatest Athletes.* Los Angeles: Tarcher, 1984.

Jensen, Peter. *The Inside Edge: High Performance Through Mental Fitness.* Toronto: Macmillan, 1992.

Mandino, Og. *A Better Way to Live.* New York: Bantam, 1991.

Peck, M. Scott. *The Road Less Traveled: A New Psychology of Love, Traditional Values, and Spiritual Growth.* New York: Simon and Schuster, 1978.

Peter, Dr. Laurence J. and Bill Dana. *The Laughter Prescription: How to Achieve Health, Happiness, and Peace of Mind Through Humor.* New York: Ballantine, 1982.

Rogers, George L. ed. *Benjamin Franklin's The Art of Virtue: His Formula for Successful Living.* 2nd Ed. Eden Prairie: Acorn, 1990.

Seligman, Martin E. P. *Learned Optimism.* New York: Knopf, 1991.

Ziglar, Zig. *See You at the Top.* Rev. ed. Gretna: Pelican, 1984.

Ziglar, Zig. *Over the Top: Moving from Survival to Stability, from Stability to Success, from Success to Significance.* Nashville: Oliver-Nelson, 1994.

Ziglar, Zig. *Top Performance: How to Develop Excellence in Yourself and Others.* New York: Berkeley, 1987.

Personal Development – Fiction

Cavicchio, Dan. *Gardens from the Sand: A Story About Looking for Answers and Finding Miracles.* New York: HarperCollins, 1994.

Chilton, David. *The Wealthy Barber: The Common Sense Guide to Successful Financial Planning.* Toronto: Stoddart, 1989.

Chopra, Gautama. *Child of the Dawn: A Magical Journey of Awakening.* San Rafael: Amber-Allen, 1996.

Clason, George S. *The Richest Man in Babylon.* New York: Signet, 1988.

Coelho, Paulo. *The Alchemist: A Fable about Following Your Dream.* Trans. Alan R. Clarke. San Francisco: HarperCollins, 1994.

Mandino, Og. *The Choice.* Toronto: Bantam, 1986.

Mandino, Og. *The Spellbinder's Gift.* New York: Fawcett Crest, 1995.

Redfield, James. *The Celestine Prophecy: An Adventure.* New York: Warner, 1993.

Redfield, James. *The Tenth Insight: Holding the Vision: Further Adventures of the Celestine Prophecy.* New York: Warner, 1996.

Leadership

Bennis, Warren. *An Invented Life: Reflections on Leadership and Change.* Reading: Addison-Wesley, 1993.

Bennis, Warren. *On Becoming a Leader.* Reading: Addison-Wesley, 1989.

Bennis, Warren. *Why Leaders Can't Lead: The Unconscious Conspiracy Continues.* San Francisco: Jossey-Bass, 1989.

Bennis, Warren and Burt Nanus. *Leaders: The Strategies for Taking Charge.* New York: Harper and Row, 1985.

Bennis, Warren and Joan Goldsmith. *Learning to Lead: A Workbook on Becoming a Leader.* Reading: Addison-Wesley, 1994.

Cooper, Robert K. and Aymen Sawaf. *Executive EQ: Emotional Intelligence in Leadership and Organizations.* New York: Penguin Putnam, 1997.

Covey, Stephen R. *Principle-Centered Leadership.* New York: Summit, 1991.

DePree, Max. *Leadership is an Art.* New York: Doubleday, 1989.

Drucker, Peter F. *The Effective Executive.* New York: Harper and Row, 1967.

Goleman, Daniel. *Emotional Intelligence: Why It Can Matter More than IQ.* Toronto: Bantam, 1995.

Goleman, Daniel. *Working with Emotional Intelligence.* New York: Bantam, 1998.

Greenleaf, Robert K. *Servant Leadership: A Journey into the Nature of Legitimate Power and Greatness.* New York: Paulist, 1977.

Kotter, John P. *Power and Influence: Beyond Formal Authority.* New York: The Free Press, 1985.

Kouzes, James M. and Barry Z. Posner. *The Leadership Challenge: How to Keep Getting Extraordinary Things Done in Organizations.* San Francisco: Jossey-Bass, 1995.

Kouzes, James M. and Barry Z. Posner. *Credibility: How Leaders Gain and Lose It, Why People Demand It.* San Francisco: Jossey-Bass, 1993.

Nanus, Burt. *Visionary Leadership: Creating a Compelling Sense of Direction for Your Organization.* San Francisco: Jossey-Bass, 1992.

Peters, Tom and Nancy Austin. *A Passion for Excellence: The Leadership Difference.* New York: Random House, 1985.

Peters, Tom. *The Pursuit of WOW! Every Person's Guide to Topsy-Turvy Times.* Toronto: Random House, 1994.

Human Spirit and Soulful Leadership

Bolman, Lee G. and Terrence E. Deal. *Leading with Soul: An Uncommon Journey of Spirit.* San Francisco: Jossey-Bass, 1994.

Handy, Charles. *The Hungry Spirit: Beyond Capitalism — A Quest for Purpose in the Modern World.* London: Hutchinson, 1997.

Hawley, Jack. *Reawakening the Spirit in Work.* New York: Simon and Schuster, 1995.

Moore, Thomas, Matthew Fox, Charles Handy, Gary Zuvak and twenty-one other contributing writers. *Rediscovering the Soul of Business: A Renaissance of Values.* San Francisco: Sterling and Stone, 1995.

Percy, Ian. *Going Deep: Exploring Spirituality in Life and Leadership.* Toronto: Macmillan Canada, 1997.

Pollard, C. William. *The Soul of the Firm.* Grand Rapids: HarperBusiness-Zondervan, 1996.

Scherer, John with Larry Shook. *Work and the Human Spirit.* Spokane: John Scherer and Associates, 1993.

Secretan, Lance H. K. *Reclaiming Higher Ground: Creating Organizations that Inspire the Soul.* Toronto: Macmillan, 1996.

Whyte, David. *The Heart Aroused: Poetry and the Preservation of the Soul in Corporate America.* New York: Doubleday, 1994.

Healing and the Mind-Body-Spirit Connection

Chopra, Depak, M.D. *Ageless Body, Timeless Mind: The Quantum Alternative to Growing Old.* New York: Harmony, 1993.

Harpur, Tom. *The Uncommon Touch: An Investigation of Spiritual Healing.* Toronto: McClelland and Stewart, 1994.

Siegel, Bernie S., M.D. *Love, Medicine and Miracles: Lessons Learned About Self-Healing from a Surgeon's Experience with Exceptional Patients.* New York: Harper and Row, 1988.

Let our website resource center
KEEP YOU GROWING!

www.clemmer.net

Visit our rich and ever-expanding Organization Transformation, Leadership Development, and Personal Effectiveness resource center on the Internet for the following:

- **Articles and excerpts.** Browse through over 200 timely articles by topic, ranging from personal development to process management!

- **Looking for inspiration? Words of wisdom?** Sign up for our complimentary Improvement Points – powerful quotes with links to full articles, delivered to you by e-mail. An excellent opportunity for personal, team, or organization development!

- **Teleconferences.** Listen to three 90-minute teleconference presentations by Jim Clemmer from the comfort of your own office! Topics include: Leadership @ the Speed of Change; Building a High Performance Culture; and Developing a Customer-Centered Organization.

- **Updates and coming events.**

- **Complimentary on-line assessments and presentations** — organizational and personal.

- **Recommended reading.** Browse through hundreds of books organized by topic area, all recommended to help you blaze your pathways to ever higher performance.

- **Site seeing.** Links to recommended sites for organizational and personal improvement.

- **Information** on The CLEMMER Group and our services.

JIM CLEMMER

Keynote Speaker and Workshop/Retreat Leader

Jim has delivered nearly 1,500 customized keynote presentations, workshops, seminars, and retreats to hundreds of leading organizations and thousands of executives. Jim is a bestselling author, workshop leader, and keynote speaker on organization improvement, leadership development, and personal effectiveness.

In addition to his many radio and television interviews, Jim has written dozens of magazine, journal, newsletter, and newspaper articles and columns. Jim is listed in half a dozen Canadian, American, and international Who's Who directories. Jim is founder and president of The CLEMMER Group Inc., a North American network of personal, team, and organization improvement experts, specialists, and consultants.

For more information on booking Jim for a keynote address, workshop, or retreat click on "Jim's Speaking" section of The CLEMMER Group's web site (www.clemmer.net) or call (519) 748-1044.

The CLEMMER Group

The CLEMMER Group provides strategic consulting services, supported by customized performance assessments, improvement and implementation planning, action-based learning workshops, and executive coaching to transform personal, team, and organization performance. Our services integrate the concepts, approaches, and frameworks from Jim Clemmer's bestselling books — *Firing on all Cylinders, Pathways to Performance,* and *Growing the Distance* — with the pragmatic, in-depth business management and professional experience of our North American network of consultants and development associates.

Services include:
Organization Assessment and Improvement Planning
Team Development
Leadership/Personal Development
Process Management
Strategic Organizational Health Services
Customer Focus
Customized Education, Training and Development

For more information on Jim Clemmer or The CLEMMER Group's services and our North American network of consultant and development associates, drop by our web site (www.clemmer.net) or call (519) 748-1044.

The CLEMMER Group Inc.
476 Mill Park Drive
Kitchener, ON Canada
N2P 1Z1

Fax: (519) 748-5813
E-mail: service@clemmer.net

Notes

CHAPTER 1 THE WAY OF THE LEADER

Page 21: "The future is not some place...," Robert Cooper and Aymen Sawaf, *Executive EQ* (New York: Advanced Intelligence Technologies, LLC: Grosset & Dunlap, Inc., a division of Penguin Putnam Inc., 1997), p. 260.

CHAPTER 2 FOCUS AND CONTEXT

Page 26: "There's only one way out...," Dan Cavicchio, *Gardens from the Sand: A Story About Looking for Answers and Finding Miracles* (New York: Harper Collins, 1994), p. 47.

Page 28: "In the early 1950s...," Joe Griffith, *Speaker's Library of Business Stories, Anecdotes and Humor* (Englewood Cliffs, N.J.: Prentice Hall Direct, a division of Arco, 1990), p. 135.

Page 28: "Carl Hiebert also used...," *A Gift of Wings: An Aerial Celebration of Canada* (North York: Stoddart, 1995), p. 31.

Page 29: "In 1924, Thomas Watson Sr....," Thomas J. Watson Jr., *Father Son & Co: My Life at IBM and Beyond* (New York: Bantam, 1990), p. 28.

Page 33: "The 18th century Scottish poet...," Peter Hay, *The Book of Business Anecdotes* (New York: Facts on File, 1988), p. 82.

Page 33: "Most business people...," Ian Percy, *Going Deep: Exploring Spirituality in Life and Leadership* (Toronto: Macmillan Canada, 1997), p. 40.

CHAPTER 3 RESPONSIBILITY FOR CHOICES

Page 48: "Whether we rise...," Carl Hiebert, *A Gift of Wings: An Aerial Celebration of Canada*, p. 29.

Page 48: "In 1981, Carl was....," Carl Hiebert, *A Gift of Wings: An Aerial Celebration of Canada*, p. 13.

Page 48: "Life is not fair...," Carl Hiebert, *A Gift of Wings: An Aerial Celebration of Canada*, p. 29.

Page 51: "What's the world's greatest lie...," Paul Coelho, *The Alchemist* (San Francisco: Harper Collins, 1993), p. 18.

Page 54: "Holding onto destructive...," Doc Lew Childre, *Freeze-Frame: Fast Action Stress Relief* (Boulder Creek, CA: Planetary Publications, 1994), p. 11.

Page 55: "Reflecting on the mounting...," Daniel Goleman, *Emotional Intelligence* (New York: Bantam Books, a division of Random House, Inc., 1995), pp 170 and 171.

CHAPTER 4 AUTHENTICITY

Page 63: "To be authentic is literally...," Warren Bennis and Joan Goldsmith, *Learning to Lead: A Workbook on Becoming a Leader* (Reading, MA: Addison-Wesley, 1994), p. 22.

Page 64: "Why the Thumb Stands...," William J. Bennett, *The Moral Compass: Stories For A Life's Journey* (New York: Simon & Schuster, 1996), p. 599.

Page 67: "Author and consultant Robert Cooper...," Robert Cooper and Aymen Sawaf, *Executive EQ*, pp. xxi, 65, and 134.

Page 68: "An entrepreneur decided...," Ashton Applewhite, William R. Evans III, and Andrew Frothingham, *And I Quote* (New York: St Martin's Press, 1992), p. 238.

Page 68: "The American Heritage Dictionary...," *The American Heritage® Dictionary of the English Language*, Third Edition (Houghton Mifflin Co., 1992), Electronic version licensed from InfoSoft International, Inc.

Page 70: "An ass found a lion's skin...," *Aesop's Fables* (New York: Avenel Books, 1912), p. 53.

Page 71: "A more contemporary storyteller...," Warren Bennis and Joan Goldsmith, *Learning to Lead*, p. 24.

Page 72: "To be honest is to be real...," William J. Bennett, *The Book of Virtues* (New York: Simon & Schuster, 1996), p. 599.

Page 72: "Seven-year-old first baseman...," *The Best of Bits & Pieces* (Fairfield, NJ: The Economics Press, 1994), pp. 91-92.

Page 75: "Hearing "reflective back talk" from friends...," Warren Bennis and Joan Goldsmith, *Learning to Lead*, p. 70.

Page 77: "According to an ancient story...," *The Best of Bits & Pieces*, p. 44.

Page 79: "In *The Heart Aroused*...," David Whyte, *The Heart Aroused* (New York: Doubleday, a division of Random House, 1994), p. 93.

Page 79: "Gautama Chopra elaborates...," Gautama Chopra, *Child of the Dawn: A Magical Journey of Awakening* (San Rafael, CA: Amber-Allen Publishing, 1996), p. 138.

CHAPTER 5 PASSION AND COMMITMENT

Page 87: "Apathy and cynicism...," Harry R. Moody and David Carroll, *The Five Stages of the Soul: Charting the Spiritual Passages That Shape Our Lives* (New York: Doubleday, 1997), p. 56.

Page 92: "During the 1980s, the Milliken...," Story told by Larry Schein, director of The Conference Board's TQM Center at the "Benchmark II" home builder conference in Scottsdale, AZ on November 7, 1994.

Page 94: "Hang in there!...," William J. Bennett, *The Moral Compass: Stories For A Life's Journey*, p. 527.

Page 94: "In 1914 Thomas Edison's factory...," *The Best of Bits & Pieces*, pp. 137-138.

Page 97: "The bedrock of character...," Daniel Goleman, *Emotional Intelligence*, p. 285.

Page 97: "During the 1960s, psychologist....," Daniel Goldman, *Emotional Intelligence*, pp. 80-83.

Page 98: "In *The Road Less Traveled*...," M. Scott Peck, M.D., *The Road Less Traveled* (New York: Simon & Schuster, 1985), pp. 15-16, 19, and 24.

Page 101: "Passion is the key element...," *Fortune*, "America's Most Admired Companies," March 2, 1998, p. 82.

CHAPTER 6 SPIRIT AND MEANING

Page 103: "Our responsibility as individuals...," Dorothy E. Fischer, "The System Versus the Soul", *Rediscovering the Soul of Business*, edited by Bill DeFoore and John Renesch (San Francisco: Sterling & Stone, 1995), p. 189.

Page 105: "In Leading with Soul:...," Lee Bolman and Terrence Deal, *Leading with Soul: An Uncommon Journey of Spirit* (San Francisco: Jossey-Bass, 1995), p. 39.

Page 109: "What most people want...," *The Best of Bits & Pieces*, p. 116.

Page 110: "At the third level...," Ian Percy, *Going Deep: Exploring Spirituality in Life and Leadership*, p. 56.

Page 111: "Everyone has a special...," Gautama Chopra, *Child of the Dawn: A Magical Journey of Awakening*, p. 150.

Page 114: "During the past few months...," M. Scott Peck, *The Road Less Traveled*, pp. 81 and 82.

Page 117: "By changing our beliefs...," Gautama Chopra, *Child of the Dawn: A Magical Journey of Awakening*, p. 138.

Page 119: "An essential factor in leadership...," Warren Bennis and Joan Goldsmith, *Learning to Lead*, p. 104.

CHAPTER 7 GROWING AND DEVELOPING

Page 126: "Isador Isaac Rabi...," *The Best of Bits & Pieces*, p. 56.

Page 127: "I am too old to change...," Vincent Barry, *The Dog Ate My Homework,* (Kansas City: Andrews and McMeel, 1997), pp. 128-129.

Page 131: "The famed ancient Greek...," *The Best of Bits & Pieces*, p. 57.

Page 131: "Scottish author Samual Smiles...," Peter Hay, *The Book of Business Anecdotes*, p. 171.

Page 132: "In a small pub...," *The Best of Bits & Pieces*, p. 127.

Page 135: "A true Master is...," Neale Donald Walsch, *Conversations with God: An Uncommon Dialogue, Book 1* (New York: G.P. Putnam's Sons, 1995), p. 114.

Page 138: "Contrary to the myth that...," James M. Kouzes and Barry Z. Posner, *The Leadership Challenge — How to Keep Getting Extraordinary Things Done in Organizations* (San Francisco: Jossey-Bass, 1995), pp. xx, xxiii, and 16.

Page 140: "Warren Bennis has studied...," Warren Bennis and Joan Goldsmith, *Learning to Lead*, p. 52.

Page 143: "With self-knowledge we lay...," Vincent Barry, *The Dog Ate My Homework*, p. 143.

Page 143: "Self-reflection is the first key...," Warren Bennis and Joan Goldsmith, *Learning to Lead*, pp. 70 and 132.

CHAPTER 8 MOBILIZING AND ENERGIZING

Page 145: "You never know when someone...," *The Best of Bits & Pieces*, p. 55.

Page 149: "After six years at Universal...," James C. Collins and Jerry Porras, *Built to Last: Successful Habits of Visionary Companies* (New York: Harper Collins, 1994), p. 39.

Page 153: "Meaningless work that...," "Reshaping an Industry: Lockheed Martin's Survival Story", *Harvard Business Review*, May-June 1997, page 93.

Page 156: "Here are some of the factors...," Daniel Goleman, *Emotional Intelligence*, p. 34.

Page 157: "A well researched book...," Daniel Goleman, *Emotional Intelligence*, p. 34.

Page 157: "This is overly conservative...," Robert Cooper and Aymen Sawaf, *Executive EQ*, p. xii and xxv.

Page 158: "If you ask people...," Warren Bennis, *An Invented Life: Reflections on Leadership and Change*, (Reading, MA: Addison-Wesley, 1993), p. 75.

Page 163: "We believe that what is...," James M. Kouzes and Barry Z. Posner, *The Leadership Challenge*, p. 40.

Page 166: "A certain man had several sons...," *Aesop's Fables*, p. 49.

AFTERWORD

Page 169: "Mr. Meant-To has a comrade...," William J. Bennett, *The Book of Virtues*, p. 364.

Page 175: "The process of spiritual growth...," M. Scott Peck, *The Road Less Traveled*, p. 266.

Page 175: "A timeless principle...," *Speakers Sourcebook II*, Glenn Van Ekeren, (Paramus NJ: Prentice Hall, 1994), p. 234.

Page 176: "Continuous personal improvement...," John Train, editor, *Wit: The Best Things Ever Said*, (New York: Harper Collins, 1991), p. 44.

Page 177: "There are no quick...," David Whyte, *The Heart Aroused*, (New York: Doubleday, 1994), pp. 87 and 89.

Index